125 best
Soup recipes

125 best Soup recipes

Marilyn Crowley & Joan Mackie

Robert
ROSE

For complete cataloguing information, see page 184.

Disclaimer
The recipes in this book have been carefully tested by our kitchen and our tasters.
To the best of our knowledge, they are safe and nutritious for ordinary use and
users. For those people with food or other allergies, or who have special food
requirements or health issues, please read the suggested contents of each recipe
carefully and determine whether or not they may create a problem for you. All
recipes are used at the risk of the consumer.

We cannot be responsible for any hazards, loss or damage that may occur as
a result of any recipe use.

For those with special needs, allergies, requirements or health problems, in the
event of any doubt, please contact your medical adviser prior to the use of any recipe.

Managing Editor: Peter Matthews
Index: Barbara Schon
Design and production: PageWave Graphics Inc.
Cover design and art direction: PageWave Graphics Inc.
Photography: Mark T. Shapiro
Inside photography, art direction: Sharon Matthews
Food Styling: Kate Bush
Props Styling: Charlene Erricson

Front cover image:
Chunky Summer Vegetable Soup with Romano Curls (see recipe, page 72).

The publisher would like to express their appreciation to the following supplier
of props used in the food photography:

Caban
396 St. Clair Avenue West
Toronto, Ontario M5P 3N3
Tel: (416) 654-3316
www.caban.ca

We acknowledge the financial support of the Government of Canada through
the Book Publishing Industry Development Program (BPIDP) for our publishing
activities.

Published by Robert Rose Inc.
120 Eglinton Avenue East, Suite 800, Toronto, Ontario, Canada M4P 1E2
Tel: (416) 322-6552 Fax: (416) 322-6936

Printed in Canada

1 2 3 4 5 6 7 8 9 FP 12 11 10 09 08 07 06 05

Contents

Introduction 6

The Soup Kitchen 8

Start to Finish 14

Classics and Beyond 44

Garden 62

Chowders 86

Hearty 106

Fancies 126

Coolers 144

Jump Starts 162

Index 185

Introduction

MANY WRITERS AND that elusive, anonymous source known as "an old proverb" get credited for having mused that, "Of soup and love, the first is best." Now that's a recommendation that even the most savvy modern marketer would have trouble topping. It's surely a clear indication of how popular and widespread the concept is, how universal the appeal of soup is and how important soup is deemed to be in achieving personal happiness! "Really?" you ask. "Isn't that a bit much?"

Well, think about it. A good soup does not let you down. It nourishes your heart as well as your tummy and spreads a feeling of satisfaction and contentment as each mouthful is savored and swallowed. A soup warms you up on a winter's day and cools you down in the sweltering heat of summer. After eating a bowl or more of delectable soup, you are guaranteed to feel better than before you ate it. If you desire soup in a hurry, you can quickly have it, and if, having made a pot of soup you decide to "put it on ice" until later, you can do that too. Is it possible to say that you can get all these satisfactions from love? Probably not!

For all you skeptics, perhaps the best way to prove the adage is for you to start making beautiful soups and seeing the effects they have on family and friends. Let *125 Best Soup Recipes* be your guide and inspiration; then, with time, you'll find you gain the confidence to combine your own ingredients into soups featuring your favorite foods and flavors.

With some easy-to-learn basic knowledge about soup making, you can build a wide-ranging repertoire. And the good news about soups is that it will not take days out of your life to make them. The old-fashioned image of a long-simmering stock pot, bubbling for hours — if not days — to produce a satisfying meal, is gone. Today's soups appeal to the carefree cook because they are quick to make, well suited to our speed-driven lifestyles and our desire for the freshness that fast prepping produces. This make-it-quickly method, which defines most contemporary cooking, retains the foods' best flavors and nourishing properties much more effectively than cooking for several hours would do.

There is an almost limitless number of soups waiting to be made. Some are "thin" such as stocks, bouillons and consommés; some are "thick" and created from stock and puréed vegetables or from stock and grains, pulses, rice or pastas; and some are chunky, showcasing bite-sized pieces of meat, poultry, fish and vegetables, making a meal in a bowl. Some are everyday fare while others are elegant enough for entertaining. Some are piping hot, others achingly cold; some are heavy with fats, others slimmed and trimmed. Complementary garnishes and tantalizing accompaniments provide value-added bonuses. Flavors, textures and looks all get star billing in a beautifully made soup, one that keeps you coming back for more. There's lifetime security knowing you can repeat the pleasure whenever you get the urge.

Now, that's more than you can say about love!

Marilyn Crowley
Joan Mackie

The Soup Kitchen

MAKING SOUP FROM scratch does not require expensive equipment, but life in the kitchen will be easier if you have stocked it with some basic utensils and if you keep some handy ingredients on your shelf or in the refrigerator and freezer. First the utensils:

Essential Utensils

Saucepans and pots. You need a couple of saucepans with tight-fitting lids, one of which should hold about 36 cups (9 L) for making stock. Old cookbooks from 30 or 40 years ago call these "soup kettles" but if you were to go to a store today and ask for one, you'd likely get a very funny look. The pot needs to be big enough to hold a chicken or a clutch of meat bones, as well as sufficient liquid for boiling them. You also should have a 12- or 16-cup (3 or 4 L) saucepan in which to make the soup. Also, we find a 12-cup (3 L) double boiler to be very useful for reheating soups, especially those containing cream or thickening agents, because they require the gentle heat of boiling water beneath the pan rather than the harsh heat of the stove element.

Skillets. It's hard to beat a cast-iron skillet for even, quick cooking. But it you really want to cut down on fat intake, then a nonstick pan is your best bet. (Did you know that a cast-iron skillet is the original "nonstick" because one that is well-seasoned achieves a surface that resembles modern treated nonstick pans?) Heavy-gauge stainless steel, possibly with a copper layer sandwiched between layers of steel,

is also an even transmitter of heat. We don't recommend uncoated aluminum skillets because they react badly to acidic foods, producing a disagreeable gray color. Whether cast iron, stainless steel or nonstick, the skillet should measure at least 10 inches (25 cm) in diameter. For making crêpe garnishes for soups, we like a 6-inch (15 cm) pan with sloping sides.

Flat wooden scraper. These lightweight inexpensive tools stir through finely diced vegetables so they cook evenly in a skillet and also smoothly scrape the bottom of a saucepan while you are heating a soup. They are easy to control and they mix ingredients thoroughly but gently.

Skimmer. Looking much like a large, flat metal spoon, about 5 inches (12.5 cm) in diameter, with small holes, a skimmer is the perfect utensil to remove the scum that forms on top of stock when you first get the temperature up to the boil. It is also useful for removing solids from liquids since it allows the liquid to fall through the holes while the solids remain on top.

Large spoon with long handle. When you need to stir through a simmering stock or a large pot of soup, a long-handled, large-bowled spoon is the best tool to use. It can be made of stainless steel or wood.

Strainer or colander. A nylon mesh strainer, at least 8 inches (20 cm) in diameter, is vital in separating liquids from solids and for pressing puréed soups into a bowl after they have been blended. Choose a strainer with hooks or handles to rest it on the rim of a bowl. Nylon is preferable to metal wire since it is easy to clean and it will not react with acidic foods. A colander with small holes may be used as a substitute.

Bowls. A large bowl with high sides and a capacity of 12 cups (3 L) is useful for storing soup after it has been cooked.

Storage containers for freezing soups. Lidded plastic containers in a variety of sizes will hold soups in your freezer until you're ready to use them. Just remember: don't fill them to the brim; leave room for the liquid to expand as it freezes. Here's another great (and more compact) way to freeze soup: transfer it to a resealable freezer bag, squeeze all the air out of the bag, seal it properly, cool it to room temperature, then lay it flat in the freezer. (Don't forget to label the containers or bag with the name of the soup or stock, the quantity or number of servings and the date you made it!) To thaw the soup, set the bag in a bowl in the refrigerator or on the kitchen counter. Or, if you're in a big hurry, break the flat frozen block over a sharp corner (as you would a Popsicle) and pop the pieces into a saucepan or microwave bowl.

Measuring cups. Sets of variously sized measuring cups are vital: ¼ cup (50 mL), ⅓ cup (75 mL), ½ cup (125 mL) and 1 cup (250 mL) is a good assortment to have. A 2-cup (500 mL) and a 4-cup (1 L) Pyrex, plastic or metal measure cups are also invaluable. If you can find one, an 8-cup (2 L) measure is also useful for soup making. Heatproof glass measures

make dandy containers for reheating soups in the microwave.

Sharp knives in at least two sizes. A chef's chopping knife with a wide, long sharp blade makes chopping easy; a small paring knife helps with fiddly tasks.

Measuring spoons. A set of four sizes attached on a ring will help when measuring herbs and spices. Recipes sometimes call for ⅛ teaspoon (0.5 mL); that's easily measured by using half of a quarter-teaspoon measure although more recent sets include this tiny measure. A "pinch" is about 1/16 of a teaspoon (0.25 mL).

Swivel vegetable parer. This quickly strips the peel from veggies such as carrots and potatoes and removes thin layers of zest from lemons and other citrus fruits.

Grater. A metal grater that stands alone or can be laid across a plate or bowl will help when grating vegetables or cheeses for soups or garnishes. Our favorite has a selection of grating sizes.

Chopping/cutting board. Whether wood or synthetic, a chopping board speeds slicing and dicing. It should be wiped clean with a hot soapy cloth, followed by clear water, after every use — and especially well after cutting raw meats, poultry or fish — to cleanse away all bacteria. Synthetic and plastic boards should be cleaned in the dishwasher.

Blender or food processor. Essential for making puréed soups, these are now relatively inexpensive and are useful for a variety of other cooking and baking chores. A blender produces a more silky purée than a food processor.

Can opener. Electric models are inexpensive; the hand-held type works almost as well.

Wire whisk (balloon whisk). A wire whisk with a sturdy handle and a wire bulb (about 6 inches/15 cm long) is the perfect utensil for combining ingredients in puréed soups and during reheating of soups that have been frozen and thawed. Mini-whisks are useful when blending small quantities of ingredients for sauces, marinades or dressings.

Garlic press. Metal garlic presses with small holes squish garlic buds so that the flavor is evenly distributed through a soup. They are not essential to great cooking, but many people find them useful. We have used several brands (such as the one pictured on page 113), but our favorite is a Henkel garlic press with removable inserts.

Cheesecloth. To obtain crystal clear broths, it is best to pour the finished stock through a sieve lined with several thicknesses of cheesecloth. The cloth traps impurities as well as solids and can be tossed in the garbage after use. You can find cheesecloth in the baking-supply sections of most supermarkets and in hardware stores.

Soup ladle. This is the best way to transfer soup from the pot to the bowl with the least mess. A 4-oz (125 mL) size will do, but we think a 6-oz (175 mL) ladle is better. Visit a restaurant supply store for the best selection, quality and price on kitchen equipment.

Assorted soup bowls. Soups look and taste better when served in elegant or imaginative bowls. Clear soups should be served in closed-shaped bowls with handles. (Yes, you may pick up the bowls and sip the last of the liquid!) Thick soups are best served in wide, shallow soup "plates." In all cases, set the bowls on an underplate and be sure to preheat bowls to be used for hot soups either by rinsing with boiling water just before using or by heating bowls in a 200°F (100°C) oven for 10 minutes. Chill bowls that will be used for cold soup by putting them in the freezer for 10 minutes. We often serve some summery soups in mugs or wide-mouthed glasses.

Soup Staples

The urge for a good soup can strike without warning so if your pantry holds certain staple ingredients, you'll be able to satisfy the craving quickly.

Stocks. Of course, homemade stock or broth stored in the freezer is best but in reality, how many of us will have a supply of it? Next best are canned stocks (especially Campbell Soup's "Healthy Request" broths, which are lower in salt and additives than others), followed by commercial stock powders or cubes (especially Knorr), made from concentrates of chicken, beef, fish and vegetable stocks. All of these have a long shelf life if stored according to directions on the package. We used our own homemade stocks (to which we add no salt) in creating these recipes. If you have substituted cans, cubes or powders, don't add any salt to the soup until you've tasted the soup at the end of cooking.

Frozen vegetables. Pair these with commercial stocks and you've a good head start on homemade soup, especially in deepest winter when fresh vegetables often look rather tired.

Dried staples. Noodles, pasta, rice, couscous, barley and legumes all give flavor and texture to many soups and, as a bonus, add visual interest.

Dried herbs and spices. While fresh herbs are always best, they are not always available, which is why a few dried herbs are handy to have in the soup kitchen. Dried herbs may also be used in making a bouquet garni, essential in stocks. Herbs and spices to have on hand include:

parsley, bay leaves, thyme, marjoram, rosemary, tarragon, basil, oregano, curry powder, black peppercorns and nutmeg. (Never, even if desperate, use powdered garlic; its rancid-tasting results will spoil all your efforts.)

Lemon juice. If a soup tastes good but not great, often the addition of $\frac{1}{2}$ tsp (2 mL) lemon juice, tipped in at the end of the cooking time, will perk it up. Keep a small bottle of it in the refrigerator — or, even better, a supply of fresh lemons in the vegetable crisper.

Hot pepper sauce. The venerable Tabasco sauce has been nudged over (if not entirely replaced) by hundreds of hot spicy sauce combinations; there are stores solely devoted to these vividly packaged bottles. Taste as many as you can to find which provides the combination of heat and flavor that you like best. We prefer DanT's Inferno Spiced Cayenne Pepper Sauce.

Sherry. Sometimes added to soup as a perker-upper, sherry's effectiveness depends on two things: the quality of the sherry (the better the sherry, the better the result), and a controlled amount (too much equals a salty taste). Use sipping sherry — not cooking sherry, which is heavily salted.

Quick garnishes. Garnishes provide a contrast in color and texture when sprinkled on soup and inject another complementary flavor hit. Chapter 1 (Start to Finish, pages 14 to 43) brims with recipes for great garnishes and "go-withs." But for fast results, check out this list of quickies, many of which you likely have in the kitchen just waiting to be pulled into service!

- Wrap and freeze leftover bacon; crumble on top of soups.
- Raid your crisper for sprigs of mint, parsley, watercress, dill, or celery leaves. Both pretty to look at and tasty on the tongue, the individual flavors of these garnishes make a perky addition to the top of any soup.
- Grate carrot, cheese, orange and lemon zest on top.
- Make a chiffonade garnish: Cut vegetables into thin matchstick-sized strips and store in very cold water; just before serving, cook them in a small amount of salted water or stock until tender but still firm; drain, then add to hot, clear soups just before bringing to the table. Or cut spinach or romaine lettuce into thin strips and add to the soup without cooking first. Use 1 to 2 tbsp (15 to 25 mL) per serving. The chiffonade can be made from just one kind of vegetable or several.
- Plop a dollop of sour cream, unsweetened whipped cream or crème fraîche spiked with a little grated horseradish or chopped fresh herbs on top of a bowl of soup. If you have used whipped cream for another reason and have some left over, stir in some horseradish or herbs and make small mounds, about 1 inch (2.5 cm) in diameter on a plate lined with waxed paper. Freeze and, when solid, transfer them to a resealable freezer bag. Float, frozen like an iceberg, on hot or cold soups for a fancy topping.
- Julienne strips of ham, tongue, chicken, seafood, sliced cold cuts, celery, carrot, or zucchini look pretty and taste terrific when included in soup.
- Dip thin slices of avocado in lemon juice then add to clear soups for color and a velvety texture sensation.
- Sprinkle a garnish of toasted slivered almonds or coarsely chopped hazelnuts to give puréed soup a smoky taste.
- A dollop of pesto stirred into an equal amount of sour cream makes a tasty topping for summer soup.
- Crumble potato or tortilla chips over a bowl of soup for a crunchy, salty hit.
- Float popped popcorn on corn or creamed soups.
- Snip chives with scissors or thinly slice green onions for a quick sprinkle.
- Crumble cheese such as feta, blue or Stilton into bottoms of warmed bowls for added taste and appearance.
- Lay paper-thin olive or lemon slices, radish, carrot and celery wafers on the surface.

Here we've gathered together our favorite recipes for basic stocks (where all great soups start), as well as imaginative finishing-off garnishes and have-withs, to create appealing and appetizing soups.

Start to Finish

Whole Chicken Stock 16

Cooked Poultry Stock 18

Fresh Chicken-Bone Stock 20

Ham Bone Stock 21

Beef Stock 22

Court Bouillon 24

Fish Stock 25

Light Vegetable Stock 26

Dark Vegetable Stock 27

Garlic Butter 28

Garlic Bread 29

Croutons 30

Crunchy Wedges 32

Fresh Salsa Topping 33

Parsnip Crisps 34

Sahara Snacks 36

Celestine Crêpes 37

Parsley Pick-Ups 38

Hot Pepper Rouille 39

Crème Fraîche 40

Flavored Butter Coins 41

Parmesan Shortbreads 42

Fast Focaccia 43

Whole Chicken Stock

The healing properties of chicken soup are legendary — and, at the heart of every recipe that claims to cure, you're sure to find a fresh chicken stock such as this. Using a whole chicken provides a richly flavored broth, as well as plenty of chicken meat to use in the finished soup.

Tip

Never add chicken liver to the stockpot — it imparts a bitter taste.

1	3-lb (1.5 kg) whole chicken	1
2	leeks, white and light green parts only, cut into chunks	2
3	carrots, cut into chunks	3
3	stalks celery, cut into chunks	3
2	small onions, cut into chunks	2
4	sprigs fresh parsley	4
1	sprig fresh thyme	1
4	bay leaves	4
4	whole peppercorns	4
16 cups	cold water	4 L

1. Place chicken, including neck and giblets (excluding the liver, if supplied) in a large stockpot. Add leeks, carrots, celery, onions, parsley, thyme, bay leaves and peppercorns. Pour in water, adding more if necessary, to ensure ingredients are well covered. Bring almost to a boil over high heat; do not allow to reach a full rolling boil or the stock will become cloudy. Reduce heat and simmer slowly for 2 to 3 hours, partially covered, skimming off and discarding any foam that rises to the surface.

2. Remove chicken; when cool enough to handle, use your hands to remove skin and chicken meat from bones. Wrap and refrigerate meat until ready to use in soup or use in salads or casseroles. Discard bones and skin. Cooked chicken will keep well for 2 days or can be frozen for up to 2 months.

3. Strain stock through a sieve. (For a very clear stock, line sieve with cheesecloth before straining.) Discard vegetables. Refrigerate for 8 hours or until fat becomes solid. Remove and discard fat layer just before using stock.

Thyme, parsley, bay leaf and peppercorns are the four ingredients that comprise a bouquet garni. They are classically tied together with string in a small muslin or cheesecloth bag, but actually can just be tossed loose into the stockpot.

Cooked Poultry Stock

While not quite as flavorful or clear as stock made from raw poultry or bones, this stock, which is made by using a roasted carcass, is still superior in flavor to that made from bouillon powder or cubes — as well as most canned broths — most of which contain MSG, "flavorings" and additives.

	Bones of 2 whole roasted chickens, any attached skin discarded or Bones of 1 roasted turkey, stuffing removed and any attached skin discarded	
2	leeks, white and light green parts only, cut into chunks	2
3	carrots, cut into chunks	3
3	stalks celery, cut into chunks	3
2	small onions, cut into chunks	2
4	sprigs fresh parsley	4
1	sprig fresh thyme	1
4	bay leaves	4
4	whole peppercorns	4
16 cups	cold water	4 L

1. Place bones in a large stockpot. Add leeks, carrots, celery, onions, parsley, thyme, bay leaves and peppercorns. Pour in water, adding more if necessary, to ensure ingredients are well covered. Bring almost to a boil over high heat; do not allow to reach a full rolling boil as the stock will become cloudy. Reduce heat and simmer slowly for 2 to 3 hours, partially covered, skimming off and discarding any foam that rises to the surface.

2. Strain stock through a sieve. (For a clear stock, line sieve with cheesecloth before straining.) Discard bones and vegetables. Refrigerate for 8 hours or until fat becomes solid. Remove and discard fat layer just before using stock.

Marilyn's Tip

"I learned in chefs' school that stocks should contain no salt because most recipes that use the stocks will specify the amount of salt needed to create the soup, depending on the other ingredients."

Joan's Tip

"At London's Cordon Bleu Cookery School we were taught never to add to the stockpot any ingredient that will break down (such as potatoes) or add color during cooking (such as beets)."

Fresh Chicken-Bone Stock

Professional chefs in top-notch restaurant kitchens use chicken bones for making their stock. Ask your butcher for a medley of different chicken bones, including backs.

Tips

While making this or any other good-quality stock can be time consuming, it is not complicated. If you make it in large quantities, you can freeze it in 2- or 4-cup (500 mL or 1 L) containers.

After the cooked stock has been drained, cooled and stored in the refrigerator, you'll notice that a layer of fat will form on the surface. If solid enough, this fat can be left on as a seal while the stock is stored in the refrigerator (where it will keep well for a week or more). Be sure to remove and discard the fat before proceeding with any recipe.

3 lbs	fresh chicken bones, any attached skin discarded	1.5 kg
3	carrots, cut into chunks	3
3	stalks celery, cut into chunks	3
2	onions, cut into chunks	2
4	sprigs fresh parsley	4
1	sprig fresh thyme	1
4	bay leaves	4
4	whole peppercorns	4
16 cups	cold water	4 L

1. Place bones in a large stockpot. Add carrots, celery, onions, parsley, thyme, bay leaves and peppercorns. Pour in water, adding more if necessary, to ensure ingredients are well covered. Bring almost to a boil over high heat; do not allow to reach a full rolling boil or the stock will become cloudy. Reduce heat and simmer slowly for 2 to 3 hours, partially covered, skimming off and discarding any foam that rises to the surface.

2. Strain stock through a sieve. (For a very clear stock, line sieve with cheesecloth before straining.) Discard bones and vegetables. Refrigerate for 8 hours or until fat becomes solid. Remove and discard fat layer just before using stock.

Ham Bone Stock

Bone-in hams are an expensive treat, which many families prepare only for special holiday entertaining. After the meat has been eaten, there is still an important role for the ham bone to play, for it imparts a unique flavor to soups and baked beans. Use a sharp knife to remove the meatiest bits of ham clinging to the bone. Dice ham and refrigerate or freeze; use as needed to add to soups, casseroles, eggs, potatoes or salads.

1	ham bone, most meat removed	1
1	large onion, quartered	1
3	carrots, sliced	3
2	stalks celery, sliced	2
1	sprig parsley	1
1	bay leaf	1
1	sprig fresh thyme (or ½ tsp/2 mL dried)	1
10 cups	cold water	2.5 L

1. In a large stockpot, combine ham bone, onion, carrots, celery, parsley, bay leaf, thyme and water. Bring to a boil over high heat, skimming off and discarding any foam that rises to the surface. Reduce heat and simmer for 2 hours, partially covered. Strain stock through a sieve lined with several thicknesses of cheesecloth. Refrigerate if using within 2 days or freeze in 4-cup (1 L) portions.

Beef Stock

This homemade beef stock is immeasurably superior to anything you can make from a powder or cube — or pour from a can. There's no denying that it's time consuming, but the exceptional result is worth every minute. So don't try to rush this stock. This applies particularly to roasting the bones and vegetables: be sure they are dark and well caramelized before transferring them to the stockpot because this will give the stock its rich brown color and intense flavor.

Tip

Always use cold water in the pot; hot water will produce a cloudy stock and off-flavors.

- *Preheat oven to 450°F (220°C)*

2 lbs	beef or veal shanks, cut into 1-inch (2.5 cm) pieces	1 kg
2	onions, quartered	2
1	large carrot, cut into chunks	1
16 cups	water	4 L
2	stalks celery, cut into chunks	2
4	sprigs parsley	4
1	large sprig fresh thyme (or ½ tsp/2 mL dried)	1
1	bay leaf	1
6	peppercorns	6

1. Arrange shanks around edges of roasting pan. Place onions and carrot in center. Roast in preheated oven, stirring occasionally, for 1½ to 2 hours or until very well browned.

2. Place roasted shanks, onions and carrot in a large stockpot. Deglaze roasting pan with 2 cups (500 mL) water, scraping up any brown bits stuck to the pan; add to stockpot. Add celery, parsley, thyme, bay leaf and peppercorns. Pour in remaining water, adding more if necessary, to ensure ingredients are well covered. Bring just to a boil over high heat, skimming off and discarding any foam that rises to the surface. Reduce heat and simmer slowly for 4 hours, partially covered.

3. Strain stock through a sieve. (For a very clear stock, line sieve with cheesecloth before straining.) Dice any meat to use in soup; refrigerate separately from stock. Cooked beef will keep well for 2 days or can be frozen. Discard vegetables and bones. Refrigerate stock for 8 hours or until fat becomes solid. Remove and discard fat layer just before using stock.

To clarify stock for consommé or other clear soups: Chill cooked stock after straining out the bones and vegetables and remove hardened fat that will form on the surface; transfer stock to a saucepan over low heat and, for each 4 cups (1 L) stock, add one slightly beaten egg white mixed with the well-crushed shell. (Trust us, this really works!) Bring to a simmer (do not boil) and cook for 15 minutes. Using a broad spoon or skimmer, remove the thick foam that forms and strain the stock through a sieve lined with several thicknesses of cheesecloth.

Court Bouillon

6 cups	cold water	1.5 L
2 cups	dry white wine or cold water	500 mL
1	large onion, diced	1
1	carrot, diced	1
1	stalk celery, sliced	
1	large clove garlic, slightly crushed	1
1	large sprig fresh thyme (or ½ tsp/2 mL dried)	1
1	sprig fresh parsley	1
6	peppercorns	6
1 tsp	salt	5 mL

Not really a stock in the traditional sense, court bouillon is a flavorful liquid used for poaching fish. Typically, the bouillon is discarded once the fish is cooked. But when we poach a white fish in this, we save the liquid to use as a dandy substitute for fish stock. We feel pretty proud of ourselves for getting two uses out of one effort! Unlike a stock, this bouillon is salted. So when using in a soup recipe, don't use any additional salt until you taste the soup close to the end of cooking.

1. In a large stockpot, combine water, wine, onion, carrot, celery, garlic, thyme, parsley, peppercorns and salt. Bring to a boil over high heat. Reduce heat to low and simmer slowly, partially covered, for 20 minutes. Strain bouillon through a sieve lined with several thicknesses of cheesecloth. Use bouillon in fish soups to replace fish stock. Refrigerate if using within 2 days or freeze in 4-cup (1 L) portions.

Fish Stock

The best fish stock is made from the bones, heads and trimmings (but not the skin, which is too fatty) of white fish such as snapper, bass, grouper and cod. (Avoid using oily fish such as mackerel, Arctic char, salmon or bluefish.) The gills should be removed from fish heads and the bones washed to remove any blood, which can cause a bitter flavor. Some chefs say that fish stock should be cooked quickly over high heat, but we like to simmer ours for 45 to 60 minutes to extract the maximum amount of flavor.

6 cups	cold water	1.5 L
2 cups	dry white wine or cold water	500 mL
3 lbs	bones, heads and trimmings from any white fish, skins discarded	750 g
1	large onion, diced	1
1	carrot, diced	1
1	stalk celery, sliced	
1	large clove garlic, slightly crushed	1
1	large sprig fresh thyme (or ½ tsp/2 mL dried)	1
1	sprig parsley	1
6	peppercorns	6

1. In a large stockpot, combine water, wine, fish pieces, onion, carrot, celery, garlic, thyme, parsley and peppercorns. Bring just to a boil over high heat, skimming off and discarding any foam that rises to the surface. Immediately reduce heat and simmer slowly for 45 to 60 minutes, partially covered. Strain stock through a sieve lined with several thicknesses of cheesecloth. Refrigerate if using within 2 days or freeze in 4-cup (1 L) portions.

Light Vegetable Stock

When choosing vegetables for this flavorful stock, use the freshest produce available. Scrimping on quality and freshness will produce a bland and disappointing stock that's hardly worth the effort. You can always bundle trimmings of asparagus, mushrooms, onions, carrots, green beans and celery into freezer bags and keep frozen, adding to the bag as the days go by, until you have enough to make a stock.

Tip

Most vegetables work well with this stock — except members of the cabbage family, such as cabbage, broccoli or cauliflower, which are too strongly flavored. For the same reasons, avoid using the dark-green parts of leeks.

6 cups	vegetable pieces (see tip, at left)	1.5 L
3	carrots, sliced	3
2	stalks celery, sliced	2
1	onion, quartered	1
1	leek, white and light green parts only, sliced (optional)	1
1	sprig parsley	1
1	bay leaf	1
1	sprig fresh thyme (or 1/2 tsp/2 mL dried)	1
8 cups	cold water	2 L

1. In a large saucepan, combine vegetable pieces, carrots, celery, onion, leek, parsley, bay leaf, thyme and water. Bring to a boil over high heat. Reduce heat and simmer for 20 minutes, partially covered. Strain stock through a sieve. Refrigerate if using within 2 days or freeze in 4-cup (1 L) portions.

Dark Vegetable Stock

Makes 8 cups (2 L)

Caramelized onions lend color and intense flavor to this brown stock and, whether you're a vegetarian or a die-hard meat eater, it's a delicious substitute for beef stock. Use it in hearty winter soups such as Fennel Soup with Cambozola (see recipe, page 116) and Lentil Dal Soup (see recipe, page 120) or whenever a stronger-flavored stock is needed.

Tip

Make this stock in large quantities and freeze in smaller containers. Be sure to leave a 1-inch (2.5 cm) space at the top of the freezer container to allow for expansion of the stock as it freezes. Or freeze in resealable bags (see page 9). Don't forget to label the stock before freezing, so you'll know what it is and when you made it!

2	large Spanish onions, sliced	2
3	carrots, sliced	3
2	stalks celery, sliced	2
1	sprig parsley	1
1	bay leaf	1
1	sprig fresh thyme (or ½ tsp/2 mL dried)	1
10 cups	cold water	2.5 L

1. In a large stockpot sprayed with vegetable spray or coated with oil, cook onions slowly over medium-low heat, stirring frequently, for 20 to 25 minutes or until onions are a deep golden brown. (Stirring is particularly important towards the end of the cooking time.) Add carrots, celery, parsley, bay leaf, thyme and water; bring to a boil. Reduce heat to low and simmer for 20 minutes, partially covered. Strain stock through sieve. Refrigerate if using within 2 days or freeze in 4-cup (1 L) portions.

Garlic Butter

8 oz	butter, softened (about 2 sticks or 1 cup/250 mL)	250 g
1 cup	canola oil or olive oil	250 mL
2	large cloves garlic, minced	2
2 tbsp	finely chopped fresh parsley	25 mL

Garlic butter is easy to make and store so we always make it in quantity, wrap it well and keep it chilled in the refrigerator for a few days or in the freezer for several months. Spread on bread or toast (see facing page), it's the perfect accompaniment to many soups. It is also divine when drizzled over veggies, such as cauliflower, or when used for sautéing chicken breasts.

Tip

This combination of butter and oil delivers all the wonderful buttery, garlicky taste of traditional garlic butter, but with added benefits: almost half the butter's saturated fat has been replaced with healthy monounsaturated oils; the canola oil is a rich source of Omega-3 fatty acid. If you use olive oil, the mixture is wonderfully flavorful and spreadable right from the refrigerator.

1. In a mixing bowl, stir softened butter until creamy with no lumps. Slowly stir in oil. When smooth, stir in garlic and parsley. Pour into small containers; seal. Refrigerate until firm. Butter will keep well in the refrigerator for 1 week or more; use chilled for spreading or bring to room temperature for a brushable liquid. Butter can be frozen for 1 to 2 months.

Marilyn's Tip

To make ready-to-serve garlic bread: Spread thick slices of day-old bread with garlic butter; wrap well and freeze. When you need a quick soup accompaniment, just pop the frozen slices into a toaster oven.

Garlic Bread

Preheat oven to 400°F (200°C)

1	baguette or Italian loaf	1
¼ to	garlic butter	50 to
½ cup	(see recipe, facing page)	125 mL
	Coarse or sea salt (optional)	

Bread: Thickly slice bread, diagonally if a baguette, leaving slices attached at bottom of loaf. Thinly coat both sides of bread with garlic butter. Seal loaf in aluminum foil and bake in preheated oven for 10 to 15 minutes or until loaf is heated through. Serve immediately.

Toasts: Thickly slice bread, diagonally if a baguette, cutting right through to separate slices. Thinly coat both sides of slices with garlic butter. Lay toasts in a single layer on baking sheet and bake in preheated oven, turning once, for 10 to 15 minutes or until golden brown and crisp. Serve immediately.

Boats: Slice baguette lengthwise. Cut each half lengthwise into 3 very long wedge-shaped pieces. Thinly coat both sides of slices with garlic butter. Cut each in half crosswise. Lay boats in a single layer on baking sheet. Bake in preheated oven, turning once, for 10 to 15 minutes or until boats are golden brown and crisp. If desired, sprinkle with coarse or sea salt. Serve immediately.

Croutons

Croutons were first created by thrifty cooks looking for ways to use up bread trimmings. Here we have a basic crouton recipe, with variations to provide you with an assortment of flavors to try as lively toppings for all sorts of soups. The croutons keep well, stored in tightly sealed bags in the freezer. Be sure to label them so you know what flavors you have put away. Use leftover French bread (baguette) or just about any other kind of bread, including pumpernickel, whole wheat and rye. Remember that day-old bread slices more easily than fresh.

- *Preheat oven to 350°F (180°C)*
- *Baking sheet*

| ¼ cup | melted butter or olive oil (or a combination of both) | 50 mL |
| 8 | slices bread, crusts removed and cubed (about 2½ cups/625 mL) | 8 |

1. In a bowl stir together butter or oil and, if desired, the ingredients for one of the variations below. Add bread cubes; toss until lightly coated. Spread in a single layer on baking sheet (or shallow baking dish). Bake, stirring once, for 10 to 15 minutes or until golden brown and crisp. Set aside to cool before using. If stored croutons lose crispness, spread out on a baking sheet; bake at 300°F (150°C) for 3 to 5 minutes or just until hot and crisp.

Variations

Curry: 1 tsp (5 mL) curry powder, ½ tsp (2 mL) ground cumin and 1 tbsp (15 mL) finely chopped fresh coriander

Fresh herb: 1 tbsp (15 mL) very finely chopped fresh basil and ½ tsp (2 mL) finely chopped fresh thyme

Garlic: 1 minced garlic clove and 1 tbsp (15 mL) finely chopped fresh parsley

Italian: 1 minced garlic clove and 1 tsp (5 mL) crumbled Italian seasonings

Moroccan: 1 minced garlic clove, 1 tbsp (15 mL) finely chopped fresh parsley and ½ tsp (2 mL) finely grated lemon zest

Parmesan: 2 tbsp (25 mL) freshly grated Parmesan cheese

Crunchy Wedges

Makes 64 small wedges

Pita breads, as a visit to most supermarkets proves, have gone from exotic to mainstream in recent years. They are an extremely versatile staple, and may be turned into a variety of delicious nibblers to accompany soups. Choose a recipe that will complement the flavors in the soup. Make a large batch and freeze in tightly sealed freezer bags, all well-labeled with the flavor and date for future reference.

- *Preheat oven to 350°F (180°C)*
- *Baking sheet*

2 tbsp	melted butter or olive oil (or a combination of both)	25 mL
4	small (6-inch/15 cm) pita breads	4

1. Lightly brush melted butter over both sides of pita; cut into 8 wedges. Split pieces, forming 2 thinner wedges. Place rough-side down in a single layer on baking sheet. If desired, sprinkle with the ingredients for one of the variations given below. Bake, stirring once, for 10 to 15 minutes or until golden brown and crisp. Set aside to cool before using. If stored wedges lose crispness, spread out on a baking sheet; bake at 300°F (150°C) for 3 to 5 minutes or just until hot and crisp.

Variations

Salt Lover's: Pinches of coarse or sea salt

Zippy: 2 tbsp (25 mL) finely chopped fresh coriander and pinches of cayenne

Herbed: 1½ tsp (7 mL) mixed dried herbs such as basil, oregano and rosemary

Clockwise from left:
Parmesan Shortbreads • (page 42),
Crunchy wedges • (page 32),
Parsnip Crisps • (page 34)

Fresh Salsa Topping

For a perky pepper-upper to soups, fish and meats, salsas can't be topped. They should be a bit hot and tangy and they are best served soon after making. (Have you never tasted a fresh salsa? The difference between this and the bottled variety is startling.)

Tip

Try adding a small spoonful of olive oil to the salsa and you'll make a terrific dip for tortilla chips.

3 or 4	plum tomatoes, seeded and finely diced	3 or 4
1/4 cup	finely minced sweet or red onion	50 mL
1	clove garlic, minced	1
1	small hot pepper (such as poblano or jalapeño) seeded and finely minced or 1/4 tsp (1 mL) hot pepper sauce	1
1 tbsp	chopped fresh coriander	15 mL
1 to 2 tsp	lime juice	5 to 10 mL
1/8 tsp	salt	0.5 mL

1. In a bowl stir together tomatoes, onion, garlic, hot pepper, coriander, half of the lime juice and salt. Let stand at room temperature for 30 minutes. Taste and, if desired, add remaining lime juice. Use at once or refrigerate, covered, for up to 1 day. Add a spoonful to garnish freshly made soup or to perk up the flavor of defrosted soups.

Chunky Chicken Noodle Soup • *(page 53)*

Parsnip Crisps

**Makes about
6 cups (1.5 L)**

1 lb	parsnips, peeled (about 4 or 5)	500 g
	Canola oil or peanut oil	
	Coarse or sea salt	

Originally created as a soup-topping garnish, these crisps are also great as nibblers served with a glass of wine. Depending on the season and the source, parsnips sometimes have a very high water content, which does not take well to deep frying. Be sure the parsnips you use are "dry" (storage parsnips are the best), then use paper towels to dab away any moisture evident on the strips before dropping them into the hot oil. Be diligent in this task, otherwise the strips will be soggy.

1. Using a vegetable peeler or mandolin, shave wide paper-thin slices off the length of each parsnip. Lay on paper towels to absorb moisture.

2. Heat 3 inches (7.5 cm) of oil in a deep saucepan over medium-high heat. (If you use a shallow skillet, use less oil and beware of fat spattering and catching on fire.) Fry a few parsnip slices at a time for less than 1 minute or until lightly golden and crisp. Use a skimmer to remove crisps from oil. Drain on paper towels; sprinkle with salt. Serve right away or store at room temperature for up to 1 day.

Sahara Snacks

With their fancy triangular shape, these "have-withs" are suitably elegant for serving to dinner guests. Tasty breads such as sourdough, Italian or light rye make the best base for the easy-to-prepare toppings. On the unlikely chance that any of these snacks remain uneaten, just freeze them, then reheat briefly in a 325°F (160°C) oven until crisp.

- *Preheat oven to 350°F (180°C)*
- *Baking sheet*

2 tbsp	melted butter	25 mL
2 tbsp	olive oil or canola oil	25 mL
6	slices bread, crusts removed	6

1. In a bowl stir together butter and oil; brush over both sides of bread. Cut into triangles and arrange in a single layer on baking sheet; if desired, sprinkle with the ingredients for one of the variations below. Bake in preheated oven for 15 minutes or until golden brown and crisp. Set aside to cool before serving.

Variations

Cheese and Garlic: Stir 1 minced garlic clove into butter and oil mixture before brushing. Sprinkle triangles with 1/3 cup (75 mL) finely grated Asiago or fontina cheese.

Cheese and Basil: Sprinkle with 1/4 cup (50 mL) grated Romano or Parmesan cheese and 1 tsp (5 mL) dried basil

Middle Eastern: Sprinkle with 2 tbsp (25 mL) sesame seeds and 1 tbsp (15 mL) ground coriander seed

Mayo and Chives: Instead of butter and oil, lightly spread mayonnaise on upper side only and sprinkle with snipped fresh chives

Celestine Crêpes

The idea of making crêpes used to scare novice cooks, who thought it an exotic and difficult task. With today's nonstick skillets, however, the mystique has been all but eliminated. The first crêpe poured into the pan is usually discarded because it "seasons the pan" and is generally less-than-perfect. In our kitchen, we always say that the first crêpe of each batch is "for the dog."

Tip

With one basic crêpe recipe in your repertoire, you have the foundation for an endless list of dishes. By adding herbs to the batter, you can use crêpes in place of pasta for cannelloni. By adding sugar and grated orange zest, you can make flaming crêpes suzette. Or, as in this recipe, you can add chopped parsley to the basic batter to create the foundation for the classic soup garnish known as "celestine."

3	eggs	3
1 ½ cups	milk	375 mL
1 cup	all-purpose flour	250 mL
⅛ tsp	salt	0.5 mL
1 tbsp	melted butter	15 mL
1 tbsp	cognac or brandy (optional)	15 mL
2 tbsp	chopped fresh parsley	25 mL

1. In a bowl whisk together eggs and milk. Whisk in flour and salt, then butter, cognac and chopped parsley until well mixed. Cover and set aside for 2 hours to allow flavors to blend and gluten in flour to rest.

2. Heat a 6-inch (15 cm) crêpe pan or skillet with sloping sides over moderately high heat. Coat bottom with a thin layer of butter or vegetable spray. Remove pan from heat; quickly pour in a generous 1 tbsp (15 mL) of batter near the handle. Immediately rotate pan so that batter runs to edges and coats pan thinly and evenly. Pour off any excess batter. Return pan to heat for 1 minute or until the underside of the crêpe is golden brown and the top is set and bubbly. Turn crêpe over and cook for 30 seconds or until lightly browned. Slide onto a wire rack to cool. Continue making crêpes until all the batter is used.

3. To use as a soup garnish, roll a crêpe into a tight cigarette-shaped roll. Cut crosswise into ⅛-inch (5 mm) slices. Drop 3 or 4 coils in each bowl of soup just before serving.

Parsley Pick-Ups

Parsley is one of the most popular ingredients used in cooking throughout the world. And little wonder: it's inexpensive, readily available and a great flavor-enhancer because it does not overpower the flavor of soups, stews or fish. Parsley is particularly useful as a restorative for soups that have been frozen for more than a month — at which point they lose much of their zing. These parsley combos give freshly made flavor to tired soups. The gremolata variation is especially good with vegetable soups. Use the charmoula or dill variations as an easy perk-up for fish and shellfish soups. Try the thyme variation in hearty bean and legume soups.

| ½ cup | finely chopped fresh parsley | 125 mL |
| 1 | large clove garlic, minced | 1 |

1. In a bowl stir together parsley, garlic and the ingredients for one of the variations listed below. Stir into or sprinkle over top of soup just before serving. Enjoy at once.

Variations

Gremolata: finely grated zest of 1 medium lemon

Charmoula: replace half of parsley with chopped fresh coriander; add finely grated zest of 1 medium lemon, 1 tsp (5 mL) ground cumin, ¼ tsp (1 mL) cayenne and 1 tbsp (15 mL) olive oil

Thyme: 1 tbsp (15 mL) lemon juice, ½ tsp (2 mL) finely chopped fresh thyme

Dill: 1 tsp (5 mL) finely chopped fresh dill

Hot Pepper Rouille

The traditional accompaniment to bouillabaisse (see Landlocked Bouillabaisse with Fresh Fennel and Rouille, *page 58), rouille also adds zing and pep to many other soups. It's not for the faint of heart, though; the combination of hot peppers and paprika pack a fiery punch on the palate.*

4 or 5	dried small hot red peppers	4 or 5
3	cloves garlic	3
4 to 5 tbsp	olive oil	60 to 75 mL
½ tsp	salt	2 mL
½ cup	bouillabaisse broth (see recipe, page 58) or fish stock or vegetable stock	125 mL
1 tbsp	hot paprika (optional)	15 mL
2 to 3 tbsp	fine dry breadcrumbs	25 to 45 mL

1. In a bowl cover peppers with warm water. Soak for 1 hour; drain. Place drained peppers, garlic, 4 tbsp (60 mL) of the olive oil and salt in a blender. Purée until well blended; gradually add stock. For richer flavor, more heat and extra color, add paprika. Blend in breadcrumbs, 1 tbsp (15 mL) at a time, until thick and creamy (like whipped cream). Taste and, if desired, blend in remaining olive oil.

Crème Fraîche

1 cup	whipping (35%) cream	250 mL
½ cup	full-fat sour cream	125 mL
1 to 3 tsp	freshly squeezed lemon juice	5 to 15 mL

The darling of nouvelle cuisine which swept the culinary world in the 1980s, crème fraîche has long been a staple in French cuisine. It is not only easy to make, but it keeps well (more than a week if tightly covered and well chilled) and provides a tart and tangy foundation for innovative quiches, dips and toppings. Anyone counting calories and fats should skip over this recipe and read on; this stuff is loaded with both — but worth every sinful bite! Be sure to use full-fat sour cream; the "light" or "fat-reduced" varieties will not work because of their gelatin content.

1. In a bowl stir together whipping cream and sour cream. Cover and let sit at room temperature for 6 hours or overnight. Line a strainer with cheesecloth (or coffee cone with a coffee filter). Pour in slightly thickened mixture. Cover and place in refrigerator to drain for several hours or overnight. Turn thickened crème fraîche into a small bowl; stir in lemon juice 1 tsp (5 mL) at a time. Taste between each addition, stopping when tangy enough. Covered and refrigerated, crème fraîche will keep well for up to 1 week. Stir into cold soups or dollop onto hot soups.

Flavored Butter Coins

A good supply of flavored butter coins in the freezer is the innovative cook's best friend. Slices can be cut off as needed for cooking, sautéing, and in making sauces and soups.

Tip
Fresh herbs are best; however, in cold-weather climates, they are not always available. So we try to dry our own herbs. Just before we think the first frost is about to strike, we select stems with healthy leaves still attached, then cut and tie them in bunches and hang in a dark airy place to dry. When perfectly dry, we put them in plastic bags, rub off the dried leaves, discard the stems, and label the contents. You can do this with rosemary, sage, thyme, oregano, parsley, tarragon, basil and bay leaves.

4 oz	softened butter (or 1 stick), about $\frac{1}{2}$ cup (125 mL)	125 g

1. In a bowl combine butter and the ingredients for one of the variations listed below. On a piece of waxed paper or parchment, form butter mixture into a log about 1 inch (2.5 cm) in diameter. Roll up; twist ends to help form roll. Refrigerate or freeze. To use, slice off coins about $\frac{1}{4}$ inch (5 mm) thick; place on top of steaming bowls of soup, vegetables, grilled steak or fish.

Variations

Parsley: 2 tbsp (25 mL) finely chopped parsley and 1 tsp (5 mL) lemon juice

Dill: $1\frac{1}{2}$ tsp (7 mL) finely chopped fresh dill (or $\frac{1}{4}$ tsp/ 1 mL dried), 1 tsp (5 mL) lemon juice and dash of hot pepper sauce

Spicy Lime: Finely grated zest of 1 lime, 1 tsp (5 mL) lime juice, $\frac{1}{8}$ tsp (0.5 mL) cayenne

Pesto: 2 tbsp (25 mL) pesto

Horseradish: 1 tbsp (15 mL) prepared horseradish, squeezed dry and 1 tsp (5 mL) lemon juice

Curry: 2 tsp (10 mL) curry powder

Parmesan Shortbreads

The slightly smoky flavor of rosemary permeates these shortbreads, providing a tantalizingly elusive taste sensation to accompany soups. Plan on providing guests with 3 or more per person at the table — or make these as part of an hors d'oeuvre platter to accompany pre-dinner drinks. Splurge on freshly grated Parmigiano-Reggiano for superior flavor.

- *Preheat oven to 350°F (180°C)*
- *Baking sheet sprayed with vegetable spray or lined with parchment paper*

1/3 cup	unsalted butter, softened	75 mL
1 cup	all-purpose flour	250 mL
1/4 cup	freshly grated Parmesan cheese	50 mL
1 tbsp	finely chopped fresh rosemary (or 1 1/2 tsp/7 mL crumbled dried)	15 mL
1/4 tsp	salt	1 mL
1/8 tsp	cayenne	0.5 mL

1. In a mixing bowl, cream butter with an electric mixer until smooth. In another bowl, stir together flour, cheese, rosemary, salt and cayenne. Slowly stir into butter until dough forms; roll into 1-inch (2.5 cm) balls. Using the palm of your hand, flatten each to 1/4 inch (5 mm) thick on prepared baking sheet. Bake on upper-middle rack in preheated oven for 20 minutes or until lightly browned. Cool on a wire rack. Store in an airtight container at room temperature.

Fast Focaccia

Serves 8

Using instant yeast quickens this recipe — the first rising takes only 10 minutes. But if you want to prepare this focaccia with lightening speed, purchase ready-made pizza dough, preferably from an Italian bakery, and top with olive oil and salt as described in the recipe (or your own favorite embellishments).

Tip

Hard bread flour has a high gluten content, which yields the best dough for bread. Often it is sold as "bread machine flour." King Arthur bread flour is an excellent American brand. In Canada, any all-purpose flour will do nicely. (All-purpose flour sold north of the border is much higher in gluten, thus closer to a hard bread flour, than the "softer" flour found in the United States.)

- *Preheat oven to 450°F (220°C)*
- *Large baking sheet with sides or large pizza pan, lightly oiled*

1 tbsp	instant or bread machine yeast	15 mL
1 tsp	salt	5 mL
3 cups	hard bread flour (see tip, at left)	750 mL
1 1/2 cups	very warm water	375 mL
1 tbsp	olive oil	15 mL
1/2 tsp	coarse or sea salt	2 mL

1. In a bowl stir dry yeast and 1 tsp (5 mL) salt into flour. Make a well in center of mixture and pour in very warm water. Stir until a dough forms. Turn out onto a floured surface. Knead for 8 to 10 minutes, using small amounts of additional flour as needed to keep dough from sticking. Invert mixing bowl over dough; let rest for 10 minutes.

2. Pat out dough on prepared baking sheet until about 1/2 inch (1 cm) thick. Let rise, uncovered, for 30 to 45 minutes or until doubled.

3. Using your fingers, spread olive oil over risen dough. Poke holes with index finger right down to baking sheet about 1 inch (2.5 cm) apart. Sprinkle with coarse salt. Bake on upper-middle rack in preheated oven for 15 minutes or until bread is golden. If browning unevenly, turn pan back to front and continue baking. Slide onto a wire rack to cool slightly; use kitchen shears or a long chef's knife to cut into pieces.

In the world of food, dishes are often categorized as being either classics or innovations. But there's no rule that says classics can't be updated to reflect contemporary trends — hence the name of this chapter.

Classics & Beyond

Dijon Vichyssoise 46

Parsnip Vichyssoise with Prosciutto 47

Ginger Chicken Noodle Soup 48

French Sweet Onion Soup 50

Cajun Shrimp Gazpacho 51

Minestrone 52

Chunky Chicken Noodle Soup 53

Pasta e Fagioli (Bean and Pasta Soup) 54

Shrimp or Lobster Bisque 56

Landlocked Bouillabaisse
  with Fresh Fennel and Rouille 58

Scotch Broth with Barley and Lamb 60

French Canadian Pea Soup with Ham 61

Dijon Vichyssoise

Serves 6

Summer suppers that start with a cooling bowl of vichyssoise are bound to please everyone at the table. Here, a sprinkling of chives on top adds both color and flavor to the soup. But it's the hint of mustard, which enhances the potato, that makes this recipe unique and delicious.

Tips

Leeks resemble onions but have an almost-sweet flavor all their own. Clean them thoroughly; cut in half lengthwise, then separate the rings while holding under cold running water to dislodge sand and earth. Cut off most of the deep green leaves and the root end, then slice.

It may seem strange to use baking potatoes for boiling, but they are really the best kind to use in this soup. The reason: they have a high starch content, which holds the cream in suspension, creating a silky smooth texture. (On the other hand, if you are making a soup where you want chunks of potatoes to retain their shape, you would use new red or white potatoes instead of the baking variety.)

1 tbsp	butter	15 mL
3	large leeks, white and light green parts only, sliced	3
1 tsp	Dijon mustard	5 mL
2	large baking potatoes, peeled and diced	2
3 cups	chicken stock	750 mL
1/2 tsp	salt	2 mL
1/4 tsp	black pepper	1 mL
1 cup	whipping (35%) cream or half-and-half (10%) cream	250 mL
2 tbsp	snipped chives or very thinly sliced green onions	25 mL

1. In a large saucepan, melt butter over medium heat. Add leeks and cook for 8 minutes or until softened. Stir in mustard. Add potatoes, stock, salt and pepper; bring to a boil. Reduce heat and simmer, covered, for 20 minutes or until potatoes are very tender.

2. Purée mixture in a blender or food processor. Refrigerate for 6 hours or overnight. Just before serving, stir in cream. Taste and adjust seasonings as needed. Ladle into chilled soup bowls and serve garnished with a sprinkling of chives.

Parsnip Vichyssoise with Prosciutto

Here we add a new dimension to traditional vichyssoise by substituting parsnips for some of the potatoes. The result is a sweet aromatic soup that's quite unlike any other. Try it at your next dinner party and see if your guests can identify the mystery ingredient.

Tip

Root vegetables store well for several months in a cool, dry, dark place. Be sure to cut off any leaves before storing, otherwise they will rob the edible roots of nutrition and flavor. Another storage tip: keep your potatoes and onions well away from each other; the onions send off a gas that causes potatoes to spoil prematurely.

1 tbsp	butter	15 mL
1	onion, diced	1
1	large baking potato, peeled and diced	1
1 lb	parsnips, peeled and sliced	500 g
4 cups	chicken stock	1 L
1 tsp	paprika	5 mL
½ tsp	salt	2 mL
¼ tsp	black pepper	1 mL
2 cups	whole milk or half-and-half (10%) cream	500 mL
1 oz	prosciutto, sliced paper thin	25 g
1	green onion, thinly sliced	1

1. In a large saucepan, melt butter over medium heat. Add onion and cook for 5 minutes or until softened. Add potato, parsnips, stock, paprika, salt and pepper; bring to a boil. Reduce heat and simmer, covered, for 20 minutes or until potato is very tender.

2. Purée mixture in a blender or food processor. Refrigerate for 6 hours or overnight. Just before serving, stir in milk. Cut prosciutto slices into long shreds. Taste and adjust seasonings as needed. Ladle into chilled soup bowls and serve garnished with prosciutto shreds and green onion.

Ginger Chicken Noodle Soup

Chicken noodle soup is one of the world's all-time favorites. But in this version, we've found two ways to make it (we think) even better: First, we intensify its flavor by browning the chicken and cooking it, with bone still attached, in the soup; second, we give it a hit of ginger, which perks up the broth without overwhelming the chicken flavor.

Tip

This is the perfect soup for anyone who's under the weather — the chicken broth provides its legendary therapeutic properties, while the ginger gently clears the sinuses.

1 tbsp	olive oil	15 mL
2	bone-in chicken breasts, skin removed or 4 bone-in chicken thighs, skin removed	2
1	onion, diced	1
2	cloves garlic, minced	2
1	carrot, diced	1
6 cups	chicken stock	1.5 L
2	thin slices ginger root	2
1	large sprig thyme (or $1/4$ tsp/1 mL dried)	1
1	large bay leaf	1
$1/2$ tsp	salt	2 mL
$1/4$ tsp	pepper	1 mL
1 cup	fine or medium egg noodles	250 mL
1 cup	frozen or fresh peas	250 mL
	Sahara Snacks (see recipe, page 36)	

1. In a large saucepan, heat oil over medium heat. Add chicken and sauté, turning once, for 10 minutes or until well browned, but not cooked through; remove to a dish. Add onion, garlic and carrot to saucepan; cook, stirring occasionally, for 5 minutes or until softened. Add stock, ginger, thyme, bay leaf, salt and pepper. Add chicken pieces and submerge in the soup.

2. Bring to a boil, stirring occasionally. Reduce heat to low; simmer, covered, for 25 minutes or until chicken is firm and cooked through. Remove ginger slices and discard. With a slotted spoon, transfer chicken to a cutting board; remove and discard bones. Dice chicken and return to soup. Reduce heat to a simmer. Stir in noodles; cook, covered, for 5 minutes or until just cooked. Stir in peas; cook for 5 minutes. Taste and adjust seasonings as needed. Ladle into warmed soup bowls. Serve with Sahara Snacks.

French Sweet Onion Soup

Serves 6

Traditional recipes for French onion soup often call for a thick layer of cheese and bread — the result being a very heavy starter. Here, we rely on the sweetness of Vidalia, Texas or Spanish onions to provide a delicious flavor that needs no cheese to round it out. As an accompanying treat, we suggest passing your guests a napkin-lined basket of crispy Parsnip Crisps *(see recipe, page 34).*

4 to 6	sweet onions, such as Vidalia, Texas or Spanish (about 3 lbs/ 1.5 kg), very thinly sliced	4 to 6
1 tbsp	butter	15 mL
2 tbsp	all-purpose flour	25 mL
6 cups	beef stock or Dark Vegetable Stock (see recipe, page 27)	1.5 L
¼ cup	dry red wine	50 mL
1	large sprig fresh thyme (or ¼ tsp/1 mL dried)	1
1	bay leaf	1
¼ tsp	black pepper	1 mL
¼ cup	finely chopped fresh chervil or parsley	50 mL
	Parsnip Crisps (see recipe, page 34) or Garlic Bread toasts (see recipe, page 29)	

1. In a large saucepan, melt butter over medium heat. Add onions and slowly cook, stirring often, for 35 to 45 minutes or until onions are richly browned. To prevent burning, stir more frequently as onions start to darken. Sprinkle with flour; stir until absorbed. Remove pan from heat. Slowly stir in cool stock and red wine; add thyme and bay leaf. Return to heat and bring to a boil. Reduce heat to low and simmer, covered, for 30 minutes.

2. Remove thyme sprig and bay leaf; stir in black pepper and chervil. Taste and adjust seasoning as needed. Ladle into heated soup bowls. Garnish with a sprinkling of chervil or parsley. Pass a basket of Parsnip Crisps or Garlic Bread toasts.

Cajun Shrimp Gazpacho

Serves 6

A classic summer pick-me-up originating in Spain, gazpacho has been adopted around the world, resulting in hundreds of variations. With its fresh-from-the-garden ingredients — none of which requires cooking — it has been called a "liquid salad." If your garden lacks some of the veggies listed here, substitute others. But do include the sliced olives; they give the soup its extra-special flavor.

Tip

Resist the temptation to use a food processor to chop and dice the ingredients for this recipe; nothing beats a gazpacho made with hand-cut vegetables. Be sure to dice them as small as you can.

4	medium very ripe tomatoes, seeded and diced	4
1	unpeeled cucumber, seeded and diced	1
1	medium sweet onion, diced	1
1 or 2	red bell peppers (preferably roasted) peeled, seeded and diced	1 or 2
1	green bell pepper, seeded and diced	1
1 cup	stuffed green olives, sliced	250 mL
1	clove garlic, minced	1
1 tbsp	wine vinegar or lemon juice	15 mL
½ tsp	hot pepper sauce	2 mL
½ tsp	salt	2 mL
¼ tsp	black pepper	1 mL
1	can (48 oz/1.36 L) garden cocktail tomato juice	1
¼ cup	finely chopped fresh coriander or parsley	50 mL
2 tbsp	olive oil	25 mL
12 oz	peeled cooked shrimp	375 g
1 cup	Croutons (see recipe, page 30)	250 mL

1. In a large glass or stainless bowl or pitcher, stir together tomatoes, cucumber, onion, red peppers, green pepper, olives, garlic, vinegar, hot pepper sauce, salt and pepper. Stir in juice; refrigerate, covered, for 6 hours or until chilled. Soup will keep well for 1 day.

2. Stir coriander and olive oil into soup. Taste and adjust seasonings as needed. Divide shrimp among chilled soup bowls. Ladle in soup and serve garnished with a few croutons. Pass a bottle of hot pepper sauce.

Minestrone

Like many traditional soups, minestrone has evolved over the centuries so that there are now almost as many variations as there are cooks! In all its variations, however, it is still probably the best known of a large repertoire of delicious Italian soups, and ingredients usually include a number of dried and fresh veggies and either rice or pasta. The name derives from the Latin for "hand out," and goes back to the time when monks kept pots of this soup in their kitchens for handing out to hungry travelers who knocked at the monastery door.

This version of minestrone comes from Kathy Thomas (Marilyn's sister), who lives in Colorado. Her two ravenous sons are always "hungry travelers."

1 tbsp	olive oil	15 mL
2	leeks, white and light green parts only, sliced	2
1	onion, diced	1
1	large clove garlic, minced	1
6 cups	vegetable stock or chicken stock	1.5 L
2	carrots, diced	2
2 or 3	new potatoes, peeled and diced	2 or 3
4 or 5	large tomatoes, seeded and diced	4 or 5
¼ cup	chopped fresh basil (or 1 tsp/5 mL dried)	50 mL
½ tsp	dried leaf oregano	2 mL
1	sprig fresh thyme (or ¼ tsp/1 mL dried)	1
1 cup	drained cooked chickpeas or Romano beans	250 mL
½ cup	broken pasta (such as spaghetti or fettuccine)	125 mL
2	small zucchini, sliced	2
½ tsp	salt	2 mL
¼ tsp	black pepper	1 mL
¼ cup	grated Parmesan cheese	50 mL

1. In a large saucepan, heat oil over medium heat. Add leeks, onion and garlic; cook for 8 minutes or until softened. Stir in stock, carrots, potatoes, tomatoes, basil, oregano and thyme; bring to a boil. Reduce heat and simmer, partially covered, for 20 to 25 minutes or until vegetables are cooked.

2. Add chickpeas, pasta and zucchini. Continue simmering for 10 minutes or until pasta is al dente. Stir in salt and black pepper. Taste and adjust seasonings as needed. Ladle into warmed soup bowls and serve garnished with a sprinkling of Parmesan cheese.

Chunky Chicken Noodle Soup

Tips

When dicing vegetables for this soup, make all the pieces the same size so they'll look pretty in the bowl.

Beware if you encounter a green center in a garlic clove; it may give a bitter taste to your soup. Just split clove lengthwise and discard green shoot.

If you are using canned chicken stock or one that is made from a powder or cubes, do not add any salt until the end. These commercial stocks tend to be salty; adding more could ruin your soup. If you accidentally add too much salt, just toss 2 or 3 thick slices of potato into the pot and cook them for 10 minutes, then discard. The potato will have absorbed some of the saltiness.

1 tbsp	canola oil	15 mL
1	onion, diced	1
2	carrots, sliced	2
2	stalks celery, sliced	2
1	clove garlic, minced	1
8 cups	chicken stock	2 L
2 or 3	skinless boneless chicken breasts, cut into 1/2-inch (1 cm) cubes	2 or 3
1 cup	broad egg noodles	250 mL
2 tbsp	chopped fresh parsley	25 mL
1/2 tsp	salt	2 mL
1/4 tsp	black pepper	1 mL
2	green onions, thinly sliced	2

1. In a large saucepan, heat oil over medium heat. Add onion, carrots, celery and garlic; cook for 5 minutes or until softened. Add stock; bring to a boil. While gently boiling, slowly drop chicken pieces into broth. When you've added the last piece, stir in noodles. Reduce heat and simmer, covered and stirring occasionally, for 10 minutes or until noodles are tender.

2. Stir in parsley, salt and pepper. Taste and adjust seasonings as needed. Ladle into warmed soup bowls and serve garnished with a sprinkling of green onions.

Pasta e Fagioli
(Bean and Pasta Soup)

Serves 8

Thought to originate in the rural kitchens of Sicily, pasta e fagioli is simple, hearty and thick. Today you'll find it served (usually warm instead of hot) throughout Italy — so much so that it's often described as Italy's national dish. Rebeka Moscarello, an imaginative Toronto home-cook, sometimes varies the types of beans and pasta she adds, but this is her basic recipe. If you fail to finish the pot, you'll notice that the noodles continue to take on liquid and expand, so you'll have to add more stock or water.

2 tsp	olive oil	10 mL
1	small onion, finely diced	1
1	clove garlic, minced	1
¼ cup	tomato sauce	50 mL
1	can (15½ oz/439 g or 19 oz/540 mL) romano or kidney beans, liquid drained and reserved	1
8 cups	chicken stock or water	2 L
1½ cups	tubettini or macaroni	375 mL
	Freshly ground black pepper	
¼ cup	chopped fresh parsley	50 mL
¼ cup	shaved or grated Parmesan or Romano cheese	50 mL

1. In a large saucepan, heat oil over high heat. Add onion and garlic; cook for 5 minutes or until softened. Add tomato sauce, beans, ¼ cup (50 mL) of the reserved bean liquid and stock; bring to a boil. Reduce heat and simmer, partially covered, for 10 minutes.

2. Stir in pasta; simmer, partially covered, for 12 minutes or until the pasta is al dente. Add several grindings of black pepper; stir in parsley. Taste and adjust seasoning as needed. Ladle into warmed soup bowls; garnish with shavings of Parmesan cheese.

Shrimp or Lobster Bisque

An impressive dish for discerning dinner guests, this exciting bisque is rich enough to serve as a main course. It's best accompanied by a chilled Pinot Gris wine and chunks of crusty French bread, followed by tossed baby greens and robust cheeses such as old Cheddar, Stilton and Parmigiano-Reggiano. Try a fruit dessert to round out this sensational menu.

Don't be surprised at what we do with the shells! They are chock full of flavor and add a rich essence.

6 cups	Court Bouillon (see recipe, page 24) or fish stock or water	1.5 L
½ cup	dry sherry	125 mL
1 lb	raw shrimp in shells or 1 ½ lbs (750 g) uncooked live lobster or lobster tails	500 g
2 tbsp	butter	25 mL
2	green onions, finely chopped	2
1	clove garlic, minced	1
1	carrot, finely diced	1
¼ cup	all-purpose flour	50 mL
1 tbsp	tomato paste	15 mL
½ cup	half-and-half (10%) cream	125 mL
¾ cup	whipping (35%) cream	175 mL
¼ cup	butter	50 mL
2	egg yolks	2
3 tbsp	cognac or brandy	45 mL
1 tbsp	finely chopped parsley	15 mL
1 cup	Croutons (see recipe, page 30)	250 mL

1. In a large saucepan, bring Court Bouillon and sherry to a boil over high heat. Add shrimp or lobster and boil briskly, 4 minutes for shrimp and 12 minutes for lobster, skimming off any foam that rises to the surface. With a slotted spoon, transfer shrimp or lobster to a plate. Set broth aside.

2. In a large saucepan, melt 2 tbsp (25 mL) butter over low heat. Add onions, garlic and carrot; cook, covered, for 3 minutes or until softened. Sprinkle with flour; stir until absorbed. Slide pan off heat. Slowly stir in tomato paste, then reserved broth; bring to a boil, stirring often. Reduce heat and simmer, covered, for 30 minutes. Stir in half-and-half cream and ½ cup (125 mL) of the whipping cream.

3. Meanwhile, shell and thinly slice about a third of the shrimp or lobster; set aside in refrigerator. Coarsely chop remaining shrimp or lobster, including the shells. In a blender or food processor, cream $\frac{1}{4}$ cup (50 mL) butter. Add chopped shellfish, including chopped shells, and 1 cup (250 mL) soup. Purée until very creamy. Rub mixture through a fine sieve. Discard contents of sieve after forcing through most of the mixture. Slowly add mixture to soup, stirring constantly.

4. In a small bowl, whisk egg yolks with remaining whipping cream and cognac. Whisking constantly, ladle in $\frac{1}{2}$ cup (125 mL) hot soup; then whisk mixture back into hot soup. Stir in reserved sliced shrimp or lobster and parsley. Taste and adjust seasoning as needed. Ladle into heated soup bowls and sprinkle with Croutons.

Landlocked Bouillabaisse with Fresh Fennel and Rouille

Serves 4 to 6

Like minestrone, bouillabaisse has as many versions as there are cooks. But culinary purists will tell you that the definitive bouillabaisse is made in the Marseilles region of southern France, using fish freshly caught and brought immediately into port by local fishermen. This recipe combines all the ingredients essential to a classic bouillabaisse and, notwithstanding our distance from Marseilles, it still tastes great.

Tip

Fiery hot rouille is a traditional accompaniment to this soup, so be sure to take the time and trouble to prepare it.

1/4 cup	olive oil	50 mL
3	cloves garlic, minced	3
1	small onion, sliced	1
3	leeks, white and light green parts only, sliced	3
3	ripe tomatoes, peeled, seeded and diced	3
1/2 cup	chopped fresh fennel or 1 tsp (5 mL) fennel seed	125 mL
1	2-inch (5 cm) strip orange zest	1
1	large sprig fresh thyme	1
1 tsp	salt	5 mL
1/2 tsp	black pepper	2 mL
1/8 tsp	crumbled saffron threads	0.5 mL
1 cup	dry white wine	250 mL
2 lbs	firm-fleshed fish fillets, (various types such as red snapper, monkfish or halibut), cut into 1-inch (2.5 cm) pieces	1 kg
1 lb	whole lobster or lobster tail or uncooked shelled large shrimp	500 g
	Boiling water	
1 lb	mussels or clams, scrubbed	500 g
1 lb	delicate-fleshed fish fillets (various types such as sole, flounder or turbot), cut into 1-inch (2.5 cm) pieces	500 g
4 to 6	slices French bread, 1 inch (2.5 cm) thick	4 to 6
1 cup	Hot Pepper Rouille (see recipe, page 39)	250 m
1/4 cup	chopped fresh parsley	50 mL

1. In a large saucepan, heat oil over medium heat. Stir in garlic, onion and leeks; cook for 8 minutes or until onion has softened. Stir in tomatoes, fennel, orange zest, thyme, salt, black pepper and saffron. Add wine and bring to a boil.

2. Add firm-fleshed fish fillets and lobster or shrimp. Add enough boiling water to cover generously. Boil gently for 5 minutes, uncovered. Using a slotted spoon, remove cooked fish and shellfish to a warm serving platter. Add mussels or clams to boiling soup and cover tightly; cook for 5 to 10 minutes or until shells have opened. (Discard any mussels or clams that do not open.) Add delicate-fleshed fish fillets; cook for 3 minutes.

3. Meanwhile, cut lobster into serving-size pieces. Lightly toast bread; spread one side thickly with some rouille. Using a slotted spoon, remove cooked fish to warm serving platter. Ladle broth into a large heated tureen. Sprinkle with parsley. At the table, place one piece of toast in each warm soup bowl; ladle broth over top. Pass seafood for guests to add to their soup as desired. Serve with additional rouille and crusty French bread.

Scotch Broth with Barley and Lamb

In its traditional form, this soup is made from mutton scraps and root vegetables and cooked for many hours. But here we use tastier, more tender lamb meat and bones left over from a roast, add lots more vegetables and greatly reduce the cooking time. Cut the meat from the bones of the roast and set aside; toss the bones into the pot at the beginning and add the meat at the end.

Tip

There are two types of barley: Pot barley has had its outer husk removed, is beige in color and features a pleasant nutty flavor; pearl barley is similar except that its surface is polished to a lighter color and it generally requires less cooking time.

1 cup	yellow split peas	250 mL
	Bones from 1 lamb roast; attached meat removed, diced and set aside in refrigerator until needed (see note, at left)	
1	onion, diced	1
3	carrots, diced	3
1	stalk celery, diced	1
1 cup	diced turnip or parsnip	250 mL
½ cup	pot or pearl barley	125 mL
10 to 12 cups	cold water	2.5 to 3 L
1 tbsp	Worcestershire sauce	15 mL
½ tsp	salt	2 mL
1 tsp	vinegar	5 mL
	Freshly ground black pepper	
¼ cup	finely chopped fresh parsley	50 mL

1. In a large pot, combine peas, lamb bones, onion, carrots, celery, turnip, barley, 10 cups (2.5 L) water, Worcestershire sauce and salt. Bring to a boil over high heat, skimming off any foam that rises to the surface. Reduce heat and simmer, covered, for 1½ to 2 hours or until soup is thick and peas and barley are very soft.

2. Remove bones from soup and discard. Skim fat from surface of soup and discard. Stir in reserved diced cooked lamb, salt, vinegar and a few grindings of black pepper. If too thick, thin with remaining water; stir in half the parsley. Taste and adjust seasonings. Ladle into warmed soup bowls; sprinkle with remaining parsley.

French Canadian Pea Soup with Ham

Early French Canadian explorers and woodsmen depended on this soup for its nutrition and suitability for traveling, since the ingredients (dried peas, savory and salt pork) kept well without refrigeration. All these voyageurs needed were streams of pure water (of which they encountered many) and, occasionally, wild leeks to liven the pot. We've kept the essence of the original soup but modernized it with ham and an assortment of veggies.

Tip

This is cold-weather soup at its flavorful best. Like many hearty soups, it freezes well; so make a batch ahead of time and freeze until needed.

1 lb	yellow split peas (about 2 cups/500 mL)	450 g
1	onion, diced	1
1	carrot, diced	1
2	stalks celery, diced	2
1/4 tsp	dried savory or sage	1 mL
1	bay leaf	1
8 to 10 cups	ham stock or cold water	2 to 2.5 L
1 cup	diced ham	250 mL
1/4 cup	finely chopped fresh parsley	50 mL
1 tsp	lemon juice	5 mL
	Freshly ground black pepper	

1. In a large pot, combine peas, onion, carrot, celery, savory, bay leaf and 8 cups (2 L) stock. Bring to a boil over high heat, skimming off any foam that rises to the surface. Reduce heat and simmer, partially covered, for 1½ to 2 hours or until peas are very soft.

2. Stir in ham; simmer, uncovered, for 20 minutes. Stir in half the parsley, lemon juice and a few grindings of black pepper. If too thick, thin with remaining stock. Taste and adjust seasoning as needed. Ladle into warmed soup bowls; sprinkle with remaining parsley.

We love the summer months when we can raid our gardens for the freshest and most flavorful produce and herbs to pop into the soup pot. But don't worry if there's no garden in your life — just go to a good grocer and choose the freshest, liveliest vegetables of the season.

Garden

Autumn Leek Soup 64

Fresh Tomato Soup with Cayenne Mayonnaise 65

Finnish Vegetable Soup 66

Asparagus and Leek Soup with New Potatoes 67

Very Green Asparagus Soup 68

Pea and Asparagus Soup with Fresh Tarragon 69

Oven-Roasted Vegetable Soup 70

Roasted Red Pepper Soup
    with Red Curry and Coconut Milk Swirl 71

Chunky Summer Vegetable Soup with Romano Curls 72

Roasted Red Pepper and Zucchini Soup 74

Spicy Roasted Red Pepper Bisque
    with Garlic Baguette Boats 75

Roasted Carrot and Onion Soup 76

Curried Cauliflower and Potato Soup with Chives 77

Cream of Cauliflower Soup with Stilton 78

Cream of Spinach Soup with Nutmeg and Yogurt 79

Chickpea and Spinach Soup 80

Sausage Savoy Soup 81

Garlicky Spinach and Beans in Broth 82

Sweet Onion and Tomato Soup
    with Fresh Basil Crème 83

Clear Corn Soup 84

Miso Soup 85

Autumn Leek Soup

Food writer Trudy Patterson, whose lush Ontario garden is the envy of her friends and neighbors, generously shares her bounty — and her recipe — with us. Vegetable soups are her favorites and she especially likes cooking with leeks.

Tip

Clean leeks thoroughly; cut in half lengthwise, then separate the rings while holding under cold running water to dislodge sand and earth. Cut off and discard the root end, as well as the dark green parts of the leaves, then slice.

2 tbsp	butter	25 mL
2 cups	sliced leeks, white and light green parts only	500 mL
1	large carrot, diced	1
¼ cup	all-purpose flour	50 mL
2 cups	chicken stock or vegetable stock, cooled	500 mL
1 tbsp	lemon juice	15 mL
8 oz	mushrooms, sliced	250 g
1½ to 2 cups	half-and-half (10%) cream or whole milk	375 to 500 mL
¾ tsp	salt	3 mL
¼ tsp	black pepper	1 mL
¼ cup	snipped chives or finely chopped fresh parsley	50 mL

1. In a large saucepan, melt butter over medium heat. Add leeks and carrot; cook for 10 minutes or until softened. Sprinkle in flour; cook for 2 minutes. Slide pan off heat. Whisk in stock and juice; when blended, return to heat. Add mushrooms; bring to a boil. Reduce heat; simmer, covered and stirring often, for 15 minutes or until carrot is tender.

2. Slowly stir in enough cream so soup is thinned but still coats the spoon. Stir in salt and pepper. Taste and adjust seasoning as needed. Ladle into warmed soup bowls; serve sprinkled with chives.

Landlocked Bouillabaisse with Fresh Fennel and Rouille • *(page 58)*

Overleaf:
Pea and Asparagus Soup with Fresh Tarragon • *(page 69)*

Fresh Tomato Soup with Cayenne Mayonnaise

Serves 4 to 6

Garden tomatoes seem to ripen all at the same time, often leaving us with more than we can use for salads and sandwiches. So here's a perfect way to celebrate the late-summer bounty — a fresh tomato soup, spiked first with piquant oregano or basil and then with a wake-up hit of cayenne mayonnaise. Because some herbs lose their punch during long simmering, we like to add them to soups near the end of the cooking time.

5 lbs	very ripe tomatoes (about 18 medium)	2.5 kg
2 tbsp	olive oil	25 mL
3	onions, diced	3
2	cloves garlic, minced	2
1 tbsp	finely chopped fresh basil or oregano	15 mL
1 tsp	balsamic vinegar or cider vinegar	5 mL
½ tsp	salt	2 mL
Pinch	granulated sugar (optional)	Pinch
¼ cup	light mayonnaise	50 mL
¼ tsp	cayenne	1 mL
	Freshly ground black pepper	

1. Core unpeeled tomatoes, saving juices; cut into quarters. Set aside.

2. In a large saucepan, heat oil over medium heat. Add onions and garlic; cook for 5 minutes or until softened. Add tomatoes and reserved juice; cook, covered, for 10 minutes or until tomatoes begin to give off their juice. Reduce heat to low and simmer, covered, for 35 to 45 minutes or until tomatoes are completely soft.

3. In a blender or food processor, purée soup in batches. For smoothest texture, force mixture through a sieve. Return to saucepan; stir in basil, vinegar and salt. Taste and, if too acidic, add a pinch of sugar.

4. In a small bowl, stir together mayonnaise and cayenne. Ladle soup into warmed soup bowls; garnish with a dollop of cayenne mayonnaise and a grinding of black pepper.

Chunky Summer Vegetable Soup with Romano Curls • *(page 72)*

Finnish Vegetable Soup

Silky smooth and studded with jewel-colored bits of vegetables, this soup will warm the cockles of anyone's heart on a cold winter's day, not just a Finn's. It's a favorite of Helene Wickstrom, an artist and musician who summers in a rustic cabin in New York's Adirondack Mountains and winters in Arizona, where she learned to make this delicious vegetable soup.

Tip

The first step in creating the soup is to make a roux — a combination of melted butter (or oil) and flour. The pot should be removed from the heat while cool liquid is slowly added. You'll notice that the mixture starts to thicken, a process that will continue after the pot is returned to the heat. The soup's exceptional silkiness comes from last-minute thickening with egg yolk.

2 tbsp	butter	25 mL
2 tbsp	all-purpose flour	25 mL
2 cups	beef stock, cooled	500 mL
2 cups	water	500 mL
Half	head cauliflower, cut into small florets	Half
3 or 4	small carrots, diced	3 or 4
1 cup	green peas	250 mL
½ tsp	salt	2 mL
¼ tsp	black pepper	1 mL
⅓ cup	whipping (35%) cream	75 mL
1	egg yolk	1

1. In a large saucepan, melt butter over medium heat. Sprinkle in flour; cook for 2 minutes. Slide pan off heat. Whisk in stock and water. When blended, return to heat. Bring to a boil, stirring frequently; add cauliflower and carrots. Reduce heat; simmer, covered and stirring occasionally, for 10 minutes or until vegetables are tender. Stir in peas; cook for 5 minutes. Add salt and pepper. Taste and adjust seasoning as needed.

2. Pour cream into a large warmed soup tureen; whisk in egg yolk. Whisk in half of the hot soup until slightly thickened, then stir in remainder. Ladle into warmed soup bowls.

Asparagus and Leek Soup with New Potatoes

The most eagerly awaited of spring vegetables, asparagus is the culinary reward we all deserve for having survived the long, dark winter. Divinely delicious, whether eaten hot or cold, asparagus also makes a welcome addition to delicate soups.

Tips

Here, we've paired asparagus with leeks and small, tender new potatoes and topped the soup with sour cream. Don't scrimp on the sour cream — the full-fat kind is best because the "light" type will disintegrate when it hits the hot soup.

Under cold running water, wash any sand from the delicate asparagus tops, snap off the tough bottoms and save to make Vegetable Stock (see recipe, page 26).

¼ cup	butter	50 mL
6	leeks, white and light green parts only, sliced	6
3	large cloves garlic, minced	3
8 cups	vegetable stock or chicken stock	2 L
8 to 10	small new potatoes, about 1 ½ inches (3.5 cm) in diameter, unpeeled	8 to 10
1 ½ lbs	asparagus, trimmed and cut into 2-inch (5 cm) pieces	750 g
1 tsp	salt	5 mL
¼ tsp	black pepper	1 mL
1 cup	sour cream	250 mL

1. In a large saucepan, melt butter over medium heat. Add leeks and garlic; cook for 10 minutes or until softened. Add stock and whole potatoes; bring to a boil. Reduce heat and simmer, covered, for 15 to 20 minutes or until potatoes are tender. Remove potatoes to a plate; set aside until cool enough to handle, then slice.

2. Add asparagus to soup; simmer, covered, for 10 minutes or until asparagus is very tender. In a blender or food processor, purée soup in batches; return to saucepan. Stir in salt and pepper. Cook until hot, but do not allow to boil; stir in half of the sour cream. Taste and adjust seasoning as needed. Place several slices of potato in bottom of each warmed soup bowl. Ladle in piping hot soup; garnish with a dollop of remaining sour cream.

Very Green Asparagus Soup

The secret of this "Kermit green" soup is to cook asparagus so briefly that it retains its fresh, barely cooked flavor without losing any color.

Tips

Inspect the quality of asparagus before buying. Signs of freshness include a shiny (not dull) appearance; crisp, tightly curled tops; and strong (not limp) stems.

To store asparagus in the refrigerator, cut ½ inch (1 cm) off the bottom of stems and stand the spears upright in a bowl to which you have added 1 inch (2.5 cm) water. Cover with a plastic bag.

2 tbsp	butter	25 mL
1	onion, sliced	1
1	clove garlic, minced	1
2 tbsp	all-purpose flour	25 mL
2½ cup	chicken stock or vegetable stock, cooled	625 mL
¼ tsp	cider or white vinegar	1 mL
8 oz	asparagus, stems removed, sliced	250 g
¼ tsp	salt	1 mL
⅛ tsp	black pepper	0.5 mL
½ cup	whipping (35%) cream	125 mL
1 cup	pumpernickel croutons (see recipe, page 30)	250 mL

1. In a large saucepan, melt butter over medium heat. Add onion and garlic; cook for 5 minutes or until softened. Sprinkle in flour; cook for 2 minutes. Slide pan off heat; whisk in stock and vinegar. Return to heat; bring to a boil. Add asparagus; reduce heat and simmer for 5 minutes, uncovered.

2. In a blender or food processor, purée soup in batches. Return to saucepan; stir in salt and pepper. Increase heat to medium and cook until hot, but not boiling; stir in cream. Taste and adjust seasoning as needed. Ladle into warmed soup bowls; garnish with pumpernickel croutons.

Pea and Asparagus Soup with Fresh Tarragon

Serves 6 to 8

This easy-to-make soup is lively with fresh vegetables and has a velvety smooth texture. Better yet, it's almost fat-free! A bowl of this soup is the closest thing you'll find to eating freshly shelled peas just plucked from the vine.

Tip

The slightly smoky flavor of this soup comes from tarragon — a perennial herb that grows as tall as 3 feet (90 cm) and is known to the French as the King of Herbs. Its mysterious anise flavor is often paired with poultry, veal and eggs.

2 lbs	asparagus, trimmed and cut into 2-inch (5 cm) pieces	1 kg
2 cups	fresh or frozen peas	500 mL
6 cups	vegetable stock or chicken stock	1.5 L
1 tbsp	chopped fresh tarragon	15 mL
½ tsp	salt	2 mL
¼ tsp	black pepper	1 mL
1 cup	rye croutons (see recipe, page 30)	250 mL

1. In a large saucepan over high heat, combine asparagus, peas, stock, tarragon, salt and pepper; bring to a boil. Reduce heat and simmer for 10 minutes or until asparagus is very tender. In a blender or food processor, purée soup in batches. Return to saucepan; heat until hot. Ladle into warmed soup bowls; garnish with rye croutons.

Oven-Roasted Vegetable Soup

Serves 4 to 6

Roasting vegetables brings out their best and sweetest flavors as the natural sugars caramelize in the fierce oven heat. Caramel is sticky stuff, however, so be sure to grease the pan or line it with baking parchment paper to make clean-up easier. Assertively flavored root vegetables such as carrots, parsnips and onions roast well. Potatoes and peppers never disappoint either. Plum tomatoes roast better than round ones because they contain far less water.

- Preheat oven to 450°F (230°C)
- 1 or 2 large baking pans, sprayed with cooking spray or lined with parchment paper

8	large plum tomatoes, cut in half lengthwise and seeded	8
1	large onion, peeled and cut in half	1
1	large carrot, peeled and cut in half lengthwise	1
2	parsnips, peeled and cut in half lengthwise	2
1	large red or orange bell pepper, seeded and quartered	1
3	cloves garlic, peeled	3
1 to 2 tbsp	olive oil	15 to 25 mL
3 to 4 cups	chicken stock	750 mL to 1 L
1 tbsp	chopped fresh thyme leaves (or ½ tsp/2 mL dried)	15 mL
1 tbsp	lemon juice	15 mL
½ tsp	salt	2 mL
¼ tsp	black pepper	1 mL
¼ cup	finely chopped fresh parsley	50 mL

1. Arrange tomatoes, onion, carrot, parsnips and bell pepper cut-side down on baking pans. Tuck 1 or 2 garlic cloves into center of pans; drizzle with oil. Place on top rack of preheated oven; bake for 40 to 45 minutes or until vegetables start to brown.

2. In a blender or food processor, purée roasted vegetables in batches if necessary, using stock as needed to create a smooth consistency; transfer to a large saucepan. Use some of the stock to deglaze the baking pan or scrape bits off parchment into pan, then add stock; pour over purée. Stir in enough remaining stock to thin soup. Stir in thyme, lemon juice, salt and pepper; bring to a boil. Reduce heat; simmer, covered, for 15 minutes. Taste and adjust seasoning as needed. Ladle into warmed soup bowls; serve sprinkled with parsley.

Roasted Red Pepper Soup with Red Curry and Coconut Milk Swirl

Serves 4

Here's a classic Mediterranean soup, that we've fired up with Thai curry paste and, as a counterpoint, soothing coconut milk.

Tips

Chances are you'll have some leftover coconut milk — but don't throw it out! Freeze it in ice cube trays, pop the frozen cubes into resealable bags and keep on hand to jazz up curries, soups and sauces. It makes a dandy substitute for whipping cream in soups.

Red curry paste is a great substitute for curry powder. It is available in Indian and Asian shops, as well as some supermarkets. After the container has been opened, it keeps well in the refrigerator.

- *Preheat broiler or barbecue grill*

3	red bell peppers	3
2 tbsp	butter	25 mL
1	onion, diced	1
1 tsp	Thai red curry paste	5 mL
3 cups	chicken stock	750 mL
1 cup	coconut milk or whipping (35%)cream	250 mL
½ tsp	salt	2 mL
1	green onion, thinly sliced	1

1. Under broiler or on barbecue grill, roast peppers, turning occasionally, for 15 minutes or until skins are charred black. Place in a paper bag; close and leave in bag for 10 minutes. Peel and cut in half. Reserving juice, discard the stem, skin and seeds.

2. In a large saucepan, melt butter over medium heat. Add onion; cook for 5 minutes or until softened. Stir in curry paste; cook for 3 minutes. Stir in stock, roasted peppers and reserved juice; bring to a boil. Reduce heat and simmer, partially covered, for 10 minutes. In a blender or food processor, purée mixture in batches. Return to saucepan and heat until hot. Stir in coconut milk and salt. Taste and adjust seasoning as needed. Ladle into warmed soup bowls; garnish with green onion slices.

Chunky Summer Vegetable Soup with Romano Curls

Serves 10 to12

Romano (or Parmesan) curls are easy to make — just shave a block of the cheese with a swivel vegetable peeler. Take the cheese out of the refrigerator 30 minutes before using; you'll find that the curls peel away more easily and keep their shape better than if the cheese is cold.

1 tbsp	olive oil	15 mL
2	onions, diced or leeks, sliced	2
3	large cloves garlic, minced	3
3	stalks celery, sliced	3
8 cups	vegetable stock or chicken stock or water	2.5L
2	large potatoes, peeled and diced	2
3	bulbs fennel, green fronds discarded and bulbs sliced	3
1	large sprig fresh thyme (or ¼ tsp/1 mL dried)	1
1	large head broccoli, cut into florets, stalk peeled and diced or half head cauliflower, cut into florets	1
8	plum tomatoes, seeded and diced	8
1	zucchini, cut in half lengthwise and sliced	1
¼ cup	chopped fresh basil	50 mL
2 tbsp	chopped fresh parsley	25 mL
½ tsp	salt	2 mL
¼ tsp	black pepper	1 mL
	Romano cheese curls (for technique, see note, at left)	
	Fast Focaccia (see recipe, page 43)	

1. In a large saucepan, heat oil over medium heat. Add onions, garlic and celery; cook for 8 minutes or until softened. Add stock, potatoes, fennel and thyme; bring to a boil. Reduce heat; simmer, covered and stirring occasionally, for 20 minutes or until potatoes are very tender.

2. Stir in broccoli; cook for 5 minutes. Stir in tomatoes, zucchini, basil, parsley, salt and pepper; heat until hot. Taste and adjust seasonings as needed. Ladle into warmed soup bowls; garnish with several Romano curls. Serve with a basket of Fast Focaccia, cut into pieces.

Roasted Red Pepper and Zucchini Soup

When zucchini overruns your garden — or the excess from your neighbor's mysteriously appears on your doorstep — try making this delightful soup. Thick with puréed vegetables, it keeps well in the refrigerator, getting even better with time. Because it also freezes well, you might consider doubling the recipe, saving half for future enjoyment.

This recipe comes to us from Susan Morrison, whom Ann Murray (not a singer but a friend of Marilyn) describes as the finest cook she has ever known.

1 tbsp	olive oil	15 mL
2	leeks, white and light green parts only, sliced	2
1	large onion, sliced	1
1	clove garlic, minced	1
4 cups	chicken stock	1 L
2	roasted red bell peppers, seeded and skinned (for technique, see recipe, page 75)	2
2	medium zucchini, sliced	2
1	sprig fresh thyme (or 1/2 tsp/2 mL dried)	1
1 tbsp	finely chopped fresh mint	15 mL
1 tsp	balsamic vinegar	5 mL
1/2 tsp	salt	2 mL
1/4 tsp	black pepper	1 mL
1/4 cup	Parsley Pick-Ups (see recipe, page 38)	50 mL

1. In a large saucepan, heat oil over medium heat. Add leeks, onion and garlic; cook for 8 minutes or until softened. Stir in stock, roasted peppers, zucchini and thyme; bring to a boil. Reduce heat; simmer, covered, for 15 minutes. Remove thyme sprig.

2. In a food processor or blender, purée soup in batches; return to saucepan. Heat until hot; stir in mint, vinegar, salt and pepper. Taste and adjust seasoning as needed. Ladle into warmed soup bowls; serve sprinkled with Parsley Pick-Ups.

Spicy Roasted Red Pepper Bisque with Garlic Baguette Boats

Roasting peppers enhances their flavor, making them a perfect complement to robust vine-ripened tomatoes and rich beef stock. This combination is also endorsed by your vegetable garden, since peppers and tomatoes ripen at the same time.

Tips

Don't be heavy-handed with the sherry! Much as you may like drinking it, too much can make a soup taste unpleasantly salty.

The Garlic Boats are a perfect accompaniment to this colorful soup.

• *Preheat broiler or barbecue grill*

6 to 8	large red bell peppers, about 2 ½ lbs (1.25 kg)	6 to 8
3 lbs	very ripe tomatoes (about 12 medium)	1.5 kg
1 tbsp	olive oil	15 mL
1	onion, diced	1
1	large clove garlic, minced	1
3 cups	beef stock or chicken stock	750 mL
2	bay leaves	2
½ tsp	salt	2 mL
¼ tsp	cayenne	1 mL
2 tbsp	medium or dry sherry	25 mL
	Garlic Boats (see recipe, page 29)	

1. Roast peppers, uncovered, under broiler or on grill until skins are charred black. Place in a paper bag; close and leave in bag for 10 minutes. Peel peppers and cut in half; discard skin, stems and seeds. Purée in a food processor or blender.

2. Core unpeeled tomatoes; saving juices, seed and cut into quarters. In a large saucepan, heat oil over medium heat. Add onion and garlic; cook for 5 minutes or until softened. Add tomatoes, reserved juice and stock; bring to a boil. Reduce heat; simmer, covered, for 35 to 45 minutes or until tomatoes are completely soft. Remove and discard bay leaves.

3. Purée soup in a blender or food processor. Return to saucepan and stir in pepper purée, salt, cayenne and sherry; heat until hot. Taste and adjust seasonings as needed. Ladle into warmed soup bowls. Pass hot Garlic Boats in a basket.

Roasted Carrot and Onion Soup

Roasting vegetables for this recipe takes a little time, but is worth every minute: it intensifies the flavors of the carrots and onions, giving them a deliciously smoky taste. Any leftover soup can be frozen for up to 1 month, but beyond that it (in fact, just about any frozen soup) will lose some flavor.

Tip

Chilling onions before cutting or slicing them will cut down on tears. Then, if you want to eliminate onion traces from your cutting board and hands, rub them with salt, vinegar or lemon juice.

- *Preheat oven to 375°F (190°C)*

1 ½ lbs	carrots, sliced ½ inch (1 cm) thick	750 g
1 tbsp	olive oil	15 mL
1	large Spanish or Vidalia onion, coarsely diced	1
2	large cloves garlic, minced	2
8 cups	chicken stock	2 L
1	large sprig fresh thyme (or ½ tsp/2 mL dried)	1
½ tsp	salt	2 mL
⅛ tsp	cayenne	0.5 mL
¼ cup	chopped fresh parsley	50 mL

1. In a large ovenproof skillet, heat oil over medium heat. Add onion and garlic; cook for 5 minutes or until softened. Add carrots; cook for 5 minutes or until just hot. Place skillet on top rack of preheated oven and bake for 40 to 45 minutes or until vegetables start to brown.

2. Transfer roasted vegetables to a large saucepan. Use some of the stock to deglaze skillet; pour over vegetables. Add remaining stock, thyme, salt and cayenne to saucepan; bring to a boil. Reduce heat and simmer, covered, for 20 minutes or until carrots are very tender. Remove thyme sprig; purée in a blender or food processor. Return to saucepan; heat until hot. Taste and adjust seasoning as needed. Ladle into warmed soup bowls; serve sprinkled with parsley.

Curried Cauliflower and Potato Soup with Chives

Lynne Ballou, a teacher in upstate New York, recommends preparing this soup when visiting friends and family are due to arrive at an uncertain hour. It's a cinch to reheat whenever the doorbell rings.

Tip

While cauliflower (a member of the cabbage family) has its own strong flavor, it marries well with cumin and curry powder. Check your curry powder, though: it comes in various strengths — from mild to fiery hot — so you may need to adjust the quantity. Our personal preference is Sharwoods medium-hot curry.

1 tbsp	olive oil	15 mL
1	large onion, thinly sliced	1
1 tbsp	curry powder	15 mL
1 tsp	ground cumin	5 mL
2	medium potatoes, peeled and diced	2
6 cups	chicken stock	1.5 L
6 cups	small cauliflower florets (about 1 head)	1.5 L
2	bay leaves	2
1/4 cup	chopped parsley or sliced green onions	50 mL
1/2 tsp	salt	2 mL
1/4 tsp	black pepper	1 mL
1/2 cup	sour cream or yogurt	125 mL

1. In a large saucepan, heat oil over medium heat. Add onion, curry and cumin; cook for 8 minutes or until onion has softened. Add potatoes; stir until coated with spice mixture.

2. Add stock, cauliflower and bay leaves. Bring to a boil. Reduce heat and simmer, covered, for 20 minutes or until potatoes are tender. Remove bay leaves; stir in parsley, salt and pepper. Taste and adjust seasonings as needed. Ladle into warmed soup bowls; serve garnished with a dollop of sour cream.

Cream of Cauliflower Soup with Stilton

The French have their Roquefort and the Italians have their Gorgonzola, but for this soup we've chosen crumbled English Stilton to counterpoint the creamy cauliflower. By placing the Stilton in heated bowls, then ladling on the soup, the cheese is gently melted without being totally incorporated into the liquid.

1 tbsp	olive oil	15 mL
1	large onion, sliced	1
1	large leek, white and light green parts only, sliced or 1 medium onion, diced	1
1	large stalk celery, sliced	1
¼ cup	all-purpose flour	50 mL
4 cups	vegetable stock or chicken stock, cooled	1 L
6 cups	cauliflower florets (about 1 head)	1.5 L
1½ cups	whole milk	375 mL
½ tsp	finely grated lemon zest	2 mL
¾ tsp	salt	3 mL
¼ tsp	black pepper	1 mL
4 oz	Stilton cheese, crumbled	125 g
2 tbsp	snipped chives	25 mL

1. In a large saucepan, heat oil over medium heat. Add onion, leek and celery; cook for 8 minutes or until softened. Sprinkle in flour; cook for 2 minutes. Slide pan off heat. Whisk in stock; return to heat. Bring to a boil, stirring frequently; add cauliflower. Reduce heat; simmer, covered and stirring occasionally, for 10 minutes or until cauliflower is very tender.

2. In a blender or food processor, purée soup in batches; return to saucepan. Stir in milk, zest, salt and pepper; heat until hot, but do not boil. Taste and adjust seasoning as needed. Crumble Stilton cheese into warmed soup bowls. Ladle in hot soup; serve sprinkled with chives.

Cream of Spinach Soup with Nutmeg and Yogurt

Serves 6

If you're concerned about fat and calories, don't be put off by the "cream" in this soup — because there's no cream in it! In fact, it's potatoes that give this soup its creamy texture.

Tip

Nutmeg is a common addition to spinach dishes because it counteracts any bitterness the spinach may develop during cooking. If possible, try to use freshly grated nutmeg. One of our favorite kitchen gadgets is a small metal nutmeg grater with a storage pocket for whole nutmeg. In this form, nutmeg keeps indefinitely and always tastes fresh when grated.

1 tbsp	olive oil or butter	15 mL
2	leeks, white and light green parts only, sliced	2
1	clove garlic, minced	1
1	stalk celery or fennel bulb, sliced	1
4 cups	chicken stock or vegetable stock	1 L
1 1/2 cups	peeled diced baking potatoes	375 mL
1/2 tsp	nutmeg	2 mL
1/2 tsp	salt	2 mL
1/4 tsp	black pepper	1 mL
2	pkgs (each 10 oz/284 g) fresh spinach, stems removed and leaves torn	2
1/2 cup	yogurt or sour cream	125 mL

1. In a large saucepan, heat oil over medium heat. Add leeks, garlic and celery; cook for 8 minutes or until softened. Add stock, potatoes, nutmeg, salt and pepper; bring to a boil. Reduce heat and simmer, covered and stirring occasionally, for 20 minutes or until potatoes are very tender. Stir in spinach; cook for 5 minutes, uncovered.

2. In a blender or food processor, purée soup in batches. Return to saucepan and heat until hot. Taste and adjust seasoning as needed. Ladle into warmed soup bowls; serve garnished with a dollop of yogurt.

Chickpea and Spinach Soup

Serves 4 to 6

Hearty and brimming with flavor, this quick-and-easy soup is a meal in a bowl when served with whole grain rolls or cornbread. The soup is equally good made with celery or fennel; just remember that fennel will impart a slight anise flavor to the soup — one that we find quite appealing, but others may not.

Tip

Rosemary is one of our favorite herbs. It's best picked fresh from the bush, but we'll admit that high-quality dried rosemary is almost as good. Be careful with your quantities, however, since too much can be overpowering.

1 tbsp	olive oil	15 mL
1	onion, diced	1
1	stalk celery or fennel, diced	1
2	cloves garlic, minced	2
4 cups	chicken stock or vegetable stock	1 L
1	can (15½ oz/439 g or 19 oz/540 mL) chickpeas, drained	1
½ tsp	crumbled dried rosemary leaves	2 mL
½ tsp	salt	2 mL
¼ tsp	crushed red pepper flakes	1 mL
6	plum tomatoes, seeded and diced	6
1	pkg (10 oz/284 g) spinach, stems removed and leaves torn	1
¼ cup	grated Asiago or Parmesan or Romano cheese	50 mL

1. In a large saucepan, heat oil over medium heat. Add onion, celery and garlic; cook for 8 minutes or until softened. Add stock, chickpeas, rosemary, salt and red pepper flakes; bring to a boil, stirring occasionally. Reduce heat and simmer, covered, for 15 minutes to develop flavor.

2. Stir in tomatoes and spinach; cook for 5 minutes. Taste and adjust seasoning as needed. Ladle into warmed soup bowls; serve sprinkled with cheese.

Sausage Savoy Soup

Any variety of green cabbage — Napa, smooth or curly-leafed savoy — will work beautifully in this soup. Buy whichever variety looks freshest in the grocery store.

Tip

Not much sausage is required to give this soup its special flavor. Just be careful about adding salt, since the sausage meat will often be quite salty on its own.

8 oz	chorizo, linguiça or Italian sausage, chopped	250 g
1	onion, diced	1
2	parsnips, diced	2
2	carrots, diced	2
8 cups	unsalted chicken stock or water	2 L
2	large potatoes, peeled and diced	2
1	bay leaf	1
2 to 3 cups	finely shredded green cabbage	500 to 750 mL
½ cup	chopped fresh basil or parsley or mixture of fresh herbs	125 mL
	Garlic toasts (see recipe, page 29)	

1. If present, remove casings from sausages. In a large saucepan, lightly brown sausage over medium heat. Discard any fat, leaving just a bit in the pan. Add onion, parsnips and carrots; cook for 8 minutes or until softened. Add stock, potatoes and bay leaf; bring to a boil. Reduce heat and simmer, covered and stirring occasionally, for 10 to 15 minutes or until potatoes are tender.

2. Stir in cabbage; cook for 10 minutes. Stir in basil; heat until hot. Taste and adjust seasonings as needed. Ladle into warmed soup bowls. Serve with hot garlic toasts.

Garlicky Spinach and Beans in Broth

Serves 3 or 4

1 tbsp	olive oil	15 mL
1	large clove garlic, minced	1
2 cups	chicken stock	500 mL
2	cans (each 15½ oz/439 g or 19 oz/540 mL) chickpeas, drained	2
½ tsp	salt	2 mL
¼ tsp	black pepper	1 mL
1	pkg (10 oz/284 g) spinach, stems removed and leaves torn	1

1. In a large saucepan, heat oil over medium heat. Add garlic and cook for 1 minute. Add stock, beans, salt and pepper; bring to a boil. Reduce heat; simmer, covered and stirring occasionally, for 5 minutes to develop flavor. Stir in spinach; cook for 5 minutes. Taste and adjust seasoning as needed. Ladle into warmed soup bowls.

Sweet Onion and Tomato Soup with Fresh Basil Crème

Serves 6

The perfect choice when you're pressed for time, this soup tastes like it's made with freshly picked tomatoes. No one need ever know they've come from a can!

2 tbsp	butter	25 mL
1	large Spanish onion, diced	1
4 cups	chicken stock	1 L
1	can (28 oz/796 mL) diced tomatoes, including juice	1
¼ tsp	cayenne	1 mL
½ cup	whipping (35%) cream, softly whipped	125 mL
2 tbsp	finely chopped fresh basil Crunchy Wedges (see recipe, page 32)	25 mL

1. In a large saucepan, heat butter over medium heat. Add onion and cook for 15 minutes or until lightly browned. Add stock, tomatoes (with juice) and cayenne; bring to a boil. Reduce heat and simmer, covered and stirring occasionally, for 20 minutes.

2. In a blender or food processor, purée soup in batches. Return to saucepan and heat until hot. In a bowl stir together whipped cream and basil. Ladle soup into warmed soup bowls; garnish with a dollop of basil crème. Pass a basket of Crunchy Wedges.

Clear Corn Soup

Serves 4

The vegetarians in your life will love you for making this soup! Its broth, unusually flavored with corn cobs, features an assortment of vegetables mingling together to provide color hits and flavor nuances that will appeal to discriminating palates — vegetarian or not. Healthy and sophisticated enough to appear on the menu of any high-priced spa, this soup is best prepared in late summer, when fresh corn is at its peak.

2	ears corn, husks removed	2
1 tbsp	butter	15 mL
1	onion, diced	1
1 cup	sliced leeks, white and light green parts only	250 mL
1	small red bell pepper, seeded and diced	1
2	jalapeño peppers, seeded and finely chopped	2
1	clove garlic, minced	1
4 cups	water	1 L
1	whole hot red pepper or ¼ tsp (1 mL) red pepper flakes	1
1	bay leaf	1
1	large sprig fresh thyme	1
¼ tsp	ground cumin	1 mL
¼ cup	chopped fresh coriander or basil (or a combination of both)	50 mL
1 tsp	salt	5 mL
¼ tsp	black pepper	1 mL
1 to 2 tbsp	freshly squeezed lime or lemon juice	15 to 25 mL

1. Standing cobs up on end, use a sharp chef's knife to cut kernels from cob; set kernels aside. Snap each cob in half and set aside.

2. In a large saucepan, melt butter over medium heat. Add onion, leeks, red pepper, jalapeño peppers and garlic; cook for 10 minutes or until softened. Add water, cobs, hot pepper, bay leaf, thyme and cumin; bring to a boil. Reduce heat and simmer, partially covered, for 20 minutes.

3. Remove cobs, hot pepper, bay leaf and thyme sprig; discard. Stir in corn kernels, chopped herbs, salt and black pepper. Heat until hot; add half of lime juice. Taste and, if desired, stir in remaining juice. Ladle into warmed soup bowls.

Miso Soup

You may be unfamiliar with some of the ingredients in this light, flavorful broth, but don't let that worry you — a trip to the oriental food section of a large supermarket or to an Asian grocer will yield all the ingredients you need to make it. Traditional in Japanese cooking, miso is an aromatic paste made from fermented soybeans or other grains and aged from 2 months to several years to develop its flavors. Mirin, a sweet rice wine, gives a gentle hit with a small quantity. Kombu and arame are two seaweed products used frequently in Japanese cooking; they're rich in calcium, phosphorus, magnesium, iron, protein and many vitamins.

1	1½-oz (40 g) piece kombu	1
6 cups	water	1.5 L
¼ cup	arame	50 mL
1	onion, diced	1
2	carrots, sliced	2
1	red bell pepper, seeded and diced	1
½ tsp	grated ginger root	2 mL
1 tbsp	mirin or rice wine vinegar	15 mL
¼ cup	miso	50 mL
8 oz	firm tofu, diced	250 g
½ cup	sliced mushrooms	125 mL
¼ cup	sliced green onions or snipped chives	50 mL

1. In a large saucepan, combine kombu and water; heat slowly over medium-low heat for 20 minutes or until piping hot. Do not allow to boil. Remove and discard kombu, reserving broth.

2. Meanwhile, in a bowl, cover arame with cold water and soak for 15 minutes. Drain; discard soaking water.

3. In a nonstick skillet sprayed with vegetable spray, cook onion over medium heat for 5 minutes or until softened. Add carrots, pepper and drained arame; cook for 5 minutes.

4. Meanwhile, in a saucepan, bring kombu broth to a boil; add ginger and mirin. In a small bowl, whisk some of the broth into miso until blended; stir back into broth. Add vegetable mixture, tofu and mushrooms; simmer for 5 minutes. Ladle into warmed soup bowls; serve sprinkled with green onions.

Long associated with the legendary clam-based soup, today's chowders now feature a much wider array of ingredients, including almost any meat, fowl or vegetable — all suspended in a thickened broth and seasoned with appropriate herbs. These recipes are contemporary in their variety but traditional in their consistency: thick and hearty, but without the glue-like texture so often encountered in lesser restaurants.

Chowders

Winter Barley Chowder with Lamb Sausage 88

Fresh Mussel Chowder with
   Saffron and Yukon Gold Potatoes 89

Bay Scallop Chowder with Double-Smoked Bacon. 90

Corn and Kielbasa Chowder 92

Sherried Mushroom Chowder with Swiss Cheese. 93

Wild Mushroom and Rice Chowder 94

Down-East Clam Chowder. 96

Tomato Clam Chowder 97

Dilled Two-Salmon Chowder 98

Spicy Thai Chowder with Shrimp and Coconut Milk. . . . 100

Fresh Seafood Chowder 102

Broccoli and Cheese Chowder. 103

Creamy Corn 'n' Cheddar Chowder. 104

Winter Barley Chowder with Lamb Sausage

Serves 10 to 12

This chowder is a meal in itself. Serve it with whole wheat bread and a green salad after a fine winter's day outdoors.

Tip

Don't be surprised at how much the barley swells as it absorbs the stock while cooking! Its nutty flavor mingles with the sausage spices to produce a flavorful, aromatic chowder. Cut the vegetables carefully and you'll be rewarded for your efforts: the bright colors sparkle like jewels in the otherwise beige-colored chowder. If you prefer cube-shaped color hits, just cut the vegetables in small dice rather than in slices.

12 cups	lamb stock or chicken stock	3 L
1 cup	pot or pearl barley	250 mL
1 lb	lamb or Italian sausage, casings removed and crumbled	500 g
3	large carrots, thinly sliced	3
2	stalks celery, sliced	2
1	large onion, finely diced	1
1	large red bell pepper, sliced	1
6	large mushrooms, sliced	6
1/4 tsp	black pepper	1 mL
1/4 cup	finely chopped fresh parsley	50 mL

1. In a saucepan bring 4 cups (1 L) stock to a boil; stir in barley. Reduce heat; simmer, covered, for 1 hour or until most of the liquid has been absorbed and barley is tender.

2. In a large saucepan over medium heat, cook sausage, stirring to break up meat, for 8 minutes or until browned. Drain and discard any fat that accumulates. Add carrots, celery, onion and bell pepper; cook for 8 minutes or until softened. Add remaining 8 cups (2 L) stock, mushrooms and cooked barley; bring to a boil. Reduce heat; simmer, covered, for 20 minutes or until vegetables are tender. Stir in black pepper and half of the parsley. Heat until hot. Taste and adjust seasoning as needed. Ladle into warmed soup bowls; serve sprinkled with remaining parsley.

Fresh Mussel Chowder with Saffron and Yukon Gold Potatoes

Serves 6 to 8

Always a mysterious spice, hand-picked saffron is the dried stigma of the saffron crocus. It takes 70,000 flowers to make 1 lb (500 g) of spice. No wonder it costs so much! But expense is only one reason to be parsimonious with saffron: use a little and it adds a wonderful flavor to the soup; use too much and it tastes medicinal.

Tips

Be careful with the wine: Add more than the quantity called for in the recipe and the soup will taste too salty.

To our minds, one clove of garlic adds just the right flavor to this chowder. But if you're a real garlic fiend, feel free to increase the amount.

2 lbs	mussels, scrubbed	1 kg
¾ cup	dry white wine	175 mL
2 tbsp	butter	25 mL
1	small onion, diced	1
3	leeks, white and light green parts only, sliced	3
1	clove garlic, minced	1
2 or 3	Yukon Gold or new potatoes, peeled and diced	2 or 3
1	bay leaf	1
6 cups	fish stock or water	1.5 L
½ tsp	saffron threads, crumbled	2 mL
¼ tsp	salt	1 mL
¼ tsp	black pepper	1 mL
2 tbsp	snipped chives or thinly sliced green onions	25 mL

1. Put mussels and wine in a large saucepan; cover tightly. Cook over high heat, shaking pan occasionally, for 5 minutes or until mussels open. (Discard any that do not open.) Drain mussels in a colander set over a large bowl; reserve broth. Set mussels aside until cool enough to handle.

2. In a large saucepan, heat butter over medium heat; stir in onion, leeks, garlic and potatoes. Cook for 5 minutes or until softened. Strain mussel broth into saucepan, leaving any sand behind in bowl. Add bay leaf and fish stock; bring to a boil. Stir in saffron. Reduce heat and simmer, covered, for 25 minutes.

3. Meanwhile, remove mussels from shells; discard shells. When chowder has finished simmering, remove bay leaf; stir in mussels, salt and pepper. Taste and adjust seasoning as needed. Heat until hot. Ladle into warmed soup bowls; serve sprinkled with chives.

Bay Scallop Chowder with Double-Smoked Bacon

Serves 6 to 8

4	thick slices double-smoked or regular smoked bacon, chopped	4
1	onion, finely chopped	1
1	leek, white and light green parts only, sliced	1
1	clove garlic, minced	1
1/2 cup	all-purpose flour	125 mL
6 cups	fish stock or chicken stock or clam broth, cooled	1.5 L
3 or 4	medium Yukon Gold or white potatoes, sliced 1/4 inch (1 cm) thick	3 or 4
1/4 tsp	crushed red pepper flakes	1 mL
1	large sprig fresh thyme	1
1	bay leaf	1
1 lb	bay or sea scallops	500 g
1 cup	half-and-half (10%) cream or whipping (35%) cream	250 mL
1/4 cup	finely chopped parsley	50 mL
1/2 tsp	salt	2 mL
1/4 tsp	black pepper	1 mL
1/4 cup	snipped chives or thinly sliced green onions	50 mL

1. In a large saucepan, lightly brown bacon over medium heat. Add onion, leek and garlic; cook for 5 minutes or until softened. Sprinkle with flour; stir until absorbed. Slide pan off heat. Add stock a little at a time (to avoid lumps), stirring until smooth.

2. Return saucepan to heat. Add potatoes, red pepper flakes, thyme and bay leaf; bring to a boil. Reduce heat and simmer, covered, for 20 minutes or until potatoes are tender. Add scallops and heat for 2 to 3 minutes or until just opaque. Stir in cream, parsley, salt and pepper. Heat until hot. Taste and adjust seasoning as needed. Ladle into warmed soup bowls; serve sprinkled with chives or green onions.

Joan's Tip

It seems that fish stores in North America offer just two kinds of scallops: large and small! How I wish we could buy the large, deep-sea scallops (with their coral roe attached) as I was able to do when I lived in England. Still, the soup works with almost any scallops you can find. The smaller variety, known as bay scallops, have a more subtle flavor than the bigger ones. They are usually, though not always, interchangeable in recipes. The large ones should be cut into slices if you are using them as a substitute for bay scallops. Whatever the size, they require very little time to cook and will toughen if left on the heat source for too long. They are done when they lose their translucent appearance and become opaque.

Corn and Kielbasa Chowder

Serves 4 to 6

We always know that autumn has arrived when we feel the urge to make this soup. The Kielbasa sausages provide an intense flavor (although they can be salty, so watch your seasoning). But if your family has milder tastes, you can always make the soup using wieners, which are passive in flavor but provide a similar texture.

Tip

We often take for granted that everyone understands the term "to simmer." But in the business of soup making, it's important to understand its precise meaning. So here goes: Simmering a liquid means that its temperature is slightly below the boiling point. Its surface is dotted by small gently-breaking bubbles, as opposed to the large rolling bubbles that boiling produces.

2 tbsp	butter	25 mL
8 oz	kielbasa, knockwurst or wieners, diced	250 g
1	onion, diced	1
4	stalks celery, diced	4
1/4 cup	all-purpose flour	50 mL
4 cups	chicken stock	1 L
6 to 8	unpeeled red or white new potatoes, diced	6 to 8
2 cups	corn kernels, fresh (or frozen, thawed and drained)	500 mL
1 cup	whipping (35%) cream or whole milk	250 mL
1/2 cup	chopped fresh parsley	125 mL
1/2 tsp	salt	2 mL
1/4 tsp	black pepper	1 mL

1. In a large saucepan, melt butter over medium heat; cook sausage until lightly browned. Add onion and celery; cook for 5 minutes or until softened. Sprinkle with flour and stir until absorbed. Slide pan off heat. Add stock a little bit at a time (to avoid lumps), stirring after each addition until smooth.

2. Return saucepan to heat. Add potatoes and corn; bring to a boil. Reduce heat and simmer, covered, for 20 minutes or until vegetables are tender. Stir in cream, half the parsley, salt and pepper. Heat until hot. Taste and adjust seasoning as needed. Ladle into warmed soup bowls; garnish with remaining parsley.

Sherried Mushroom Chowder with Swiss Cheese

Sherry and mushrooms are a natural combination, each complementing and enhancing the flavor of the other. Just remember that when it comes to cooking with sherry, more is not always better. (Drinking it is another matter.) Too much sherry in this soup will produce a too-salty taste.

This chowder features another winning combination: olive oil and butter. Pairing these ingredients lets loose the distinctive flavors of both.

1 tbsp	butter	15 mL
1 tbsp	olive oil	15 mL
1	onion, thinly sliced	1
2	stalks celery, sliced	2
1	carrot, diced	1
1	large clove garlic, minced	1
½ cup	all-purpose flour	125 mL
5 cups	chicken stock	1.25 L
4 to 6 cups	sliced mixed mushrooms	1 to 1.5 L
2 cups	whole milk or half-and-half (10%) cream	500 mL
1 tbsp	dry sherry	15 mL
¼ tsp	pepper	1 mL
1 cup	grated Swiss cheese (Gruyère or Emmental)	250 mL
¼ cup	finely chopped coriander or parsley	50 mL

1. In a large saucepan, heat butter and oil over medium heat. Stir in onion, celery, carrot and garlic; cook for 5 minutes or until onion has softened. Sprinkle with flour and stir until absorbed. Slide pan off heat. Add stock a little at a time (to avoid lumps), stirring after each addition until smooth.

2. Return saucepan to heat. Add mushrooms; bring to a boil. Reduce heat and simmer, covered, for 10 minutes or until vegetables are tender. Stir in milk, sherry and pepper; heat until hot. Taste and adjust seasoning as needed. Add cheese, stirring briefly until melted. (Over-stirring can make cheese stringy.) Ladle into warmed soup bowls; serve sprinkled with fresh coriander.

Wild Mushroom and Rice Chowder

Serves 6 to 8

1 tbsp	butter	15 mL
1 tbsp	olive oil	15 mL
1	onion, thinly sliced	1
2	stalks celery, sliced	2
1	large clove garlic, minced	1
1/2 cup	all-purpose flour	125 mL
6 cups	Dark Vegetable Stock (see recipe, page 27) or beef or chicken stock, cooled	1.5 L
4 to 6 cups	sliced mixed mushrooms	1 to 1.5 L
1	large sprig fresh thyme (or 1/4 tsp/1 mL dried)	1
1/4 tsp	salt	1 mL
1/4 tsp	pepper	1 mL
1 1/2 cups	cooked wild, brown or white rice (for technique, see tip, facing page)	375 mL
1/4 cup	finely shredded fresh basil	50 mL
1/2 cup	whipping (35%) cream or half-and-half (10%) cream	125 mL

1. In a large saucepan, heat butter and oil over medium heat. Stir in onion, celery and garlic; cook for 5 minutes or until onion has softened. Sprinkle with flour and stir until absorbed. Slide pan off heat. Add stock a little at a time (to avoid lumps), stirring after each addition until smooth.

2. Return saucepan to heat. Add mushrooms and thyme; bring to a boil. Reduce heat and simmer, covered and stirring occasionally, for 20 minutes or until vegetables are tender. Stir in salt and pepper; remove thyme sprig. Taste and adjust seasoning as needed. Just before serving, stir in rice and basil; heat until hot. Ladle into warmed soup bowls; serve garnished with a swirl of cream in the center.

Marilyn's Tips

My son, Paul, requests this chowder for every birthday dinner — and then puts dibs on any leftovers! I use whatever wild mushrooms I can find at my local supermarket: a mixture of cremini, button and oyster mushrooms plus a few strongly flavored shiitake.

Most of the wild rice sold in North America comes from Minnesota and Manitoba. And while much of it is, in fact, "wild" an increasing amount is cultivated. Cooking wild rice differs from cooking regular white rice. Here's how to prepare what you'll need for this chowder. Pour ¾ cup (175 mL) wild rice into a saucepan. Generously cover with water and bring to a boil. Reduce heat and simmer for 35 to 40 minutes or until tender, checking halfway through cooking time to make sure that there is still water in the pot. Drain and cool until needed.

Down-East Clam Chowder

Serves 6

"Down East," as Canada's maritime provinces are collectively known, is where you'll find many a hearty chowder like this — full of flavors redolent of the sea and often served as a simple supper along with a great loaf of homemade bread and a glass of beer. Here we've used canned clams, but if you're adventurous (or are lucky enough to live by the sea), try using a couple of pounds of fresh clams.

2	slices bacon, chopped	2
1	onion, diced	1
2	stalks celery, diced	2
4	medium carrots, diced	4
1/2 cup	all-purpose flour	125 mL
4	medium potatoes, peeled and diced	4
2 cups	chicken stock or water	500 mL
1	can (5 oz/142 g) baby clams, drained, liquid reserved	1
1	large sprig fresh thyme	1
1	bay leaf	1
2 cups	whole milk	500 mL
1/4 tsp	hot pepper sauce	1 mL
1/4 tsp	black pepper	1 mL
2 tbsp	chopped fresh parsley	25 mL

1. In a large saucepan, sauté bacon over medium heat. Stir in onion, celery and carrots; cook for 5 minutes or until softened. Stir in flour and cook for 1 minute. Slide pan off heat. Slowly stir in stock and drained liquid from clams; reserve clams. Submerge thyme and bay leaf in soup; bring just to a boil, stirring frequently. (Soup will be very thick.) Reduce heat and simmer, covered and stirring frequently, for 20 minutes or until potato is tender. Discard thyme sprig and bay leaf.

2. Stir in clams, milk, hot pepper sauce and black pepper; heat until hot, but do not boil. Taste and adjust seasoning as needed. Ladle into warmed soup bowls; serve sprinkled with parsley.

Creamy Corn 'n' Cheddar Chowder • *page 104*

Overleaf:
Dilled Two-Salmon Chowder • *page 98*

Tomato Clam Chowder

Serves 4 to 6

Tip

Rather than making do with ordinary celery, try to find fennel for this soup. Its anise flavor gives a subtle note to the chowder. Eat any that you don't use, raw like celery sticks or sliced into a salad.

1 tbsp	olive oil or canola oil	15 mL
1	onion, finely chopped	1
1	large carrot, diced	1
1	stalk celery or fennel, diced	1
1	can (28 oz/796 mL) diced tomatoes, including juice	1
4 cups	water or bottled clam juice or chicken stock	1 L
1	large potato, peeled and diced	1
1	large sprig fresh thyme	1
1	bay leaf	1
2 lbs	fresh clams or mussels	1 kg
1/4 cup	finely chopped parsley	50 mL
1/4 tsp	black pepper	1 mL

1. In a large saucepan, heat oil over medium heat. Add onion, carrot and celery; cook for 5 minutes or until onion is softened. Stir in tomatoes (with juice) and water. Add potato, thyme and bay leaf; bring to a boil. Reduce heat and simmer, covered, for 20 minutes or until potato is tender.

2. Increase heat to medium; when gently boiling, add shellfish. Cook, covered tightly, 15 minutes for clams, 8 minutes for mussels or until opened. (Discard any shellfish that do not open.) Remove thyme sprig and bay leaf; stir in half of the parsley and the pepper. Heat until hot. Taste and adjust seasoning as needed. Ladle soup, shells and all, into large wide heated soup bowls; serve sprinkled with remaining parsley.

Marilyn's Note

In the days when I worked in restaurants, I picked up many helpful tips, but one of the best was to make clam chowder on a Friday — that's traditionally when the demand for shellfish is greatest and they're at their freshest. Mondays or Tuesdays are the worst days to buy shellfish, which are usually leftovers from the previous week.

Fiery Fall Pumpkin Soup with Shrimp • page 112

Dilled Two-Salmon Chowder

Serves 4 to 6

Loaded with healthy Omega-3 fatty acids, salmon is great for the heart — and the palate. Here we've combined fresh salmon with a little smoked salmon to give the chowder a depth of flavor usually only achieved with bacon. The fresh flavor hits of lemon and dill wake up your taste buds. Use milk rather than light cream if you're watching your cholesterol.

2 tbsp	butter	25 mL
1	medium onion, diced	1
2 tbsp	all-purpose flour	25 mL
2½ cups	fish stock or water	625 mL
4	medium new potatoes, peeled and diced	4
1 lb	salmon steak or fillet, bones and skin removed, cut into 1-inch (2.5 cm) cubes	500 g
½ tsp	finely grated lemon zest	2 mL
2½ cups	whole milk or half-and-half (10%) cream	625 mL
1 tbsp	finely chopped fresh dill (or ¼ tsp/1 mL dried)	15 mL
4 oz	smoked salmon, chopped	125 g
½ tsp	salt	2 mL
¼ tsp	black pepper	1 mL
	Fresh dill	

1. In a large saucepan, melt butter over medium heat. Stir in onion and cook for 5 minutes or until onion has softened. Sprinkle with flour and stir until absorbed. Slide pan off heat. Add stock a little at a time (to avoid lumps), stirring after each addition until smooth.

2. Return saucepan to heat. Add potatoes; bring to a boil. Reduce heat and simmer, covered and stirring occasionally, for 15 minutes or until potatoes are tender. Add fresh salmon and zest; simmer for 3 to 5 minutes or just until fish is cooked. Gently stir in milk, dill, smoked salmon, salt and pepper; heat until hot, but do not boil. Taste and adjust seasoning as needed. Ladle into heated soup bowls; serve sprinkled with additional fresh dill.

Spicy Thai Chowder with Shrimp and Coconut Milk

Here's a chowder that will blow the cobwebs out of your sinuses! The heat blast comes from curry paste which, for most people, is very spicy indeed. But for those who like their food really, really spicy, serve this soup accompanied by a bottle of hot pepper sauce to pass at the table.

Tip

Are you sometimes uncertain whether the shrimp you see in the freezer sections of the supermarket or laid out on shaved ice at the fish counter are raw or cooked? Here's how to tell: if gray in color, they are raw; if pink, they have been cooked. Cooking shrimp, as with scallops, takes mere minutes. Overcooking will cause them to become tough. If shrimp are already cooked, just heat them briefly.

4 oz	thin rice stick noodles	125 g
3	green onions	3
1	stalk lemongrass	1
1 tbsp	canola oil	15 mL
2	cloves garlic, minced	2
1 tbsp	grated ginger root	15 mL
1/2 tsp	Thai red or green curry paste or crushed red pepper flakes	2 mL
6 cups	chicken stock	1.5 L
2 tbsp	fish sauce	25 mL
2 cups	sliced mixed mushrooms	500 mL
1 lb	peeled tail-on large shrimp	500 g
2 tbsp	lime juice	25 mL
1 cup	light or regular unsweetened coconut milk	250 mL
3	sprigs coriander	3

1. Place noodles in a large bowl. Generously cover with boiling water; set aside to soak while making soup. Thinly slice green tops from onions and set aside, then thinly slice white parts. Cut off about half of light-green lemongrass top and discard. Using a kitchen mallet or bottom of a heavy pot, lightly crush bottom white bulb.

2. In a large pot, heat oil over medium heat. Stir in garlic, white part of onion, ginger and curry paste; cook for 2 minutes or until very fragrant. Stir in stock, fish sauce and lemongrass, ensuring lemongrass is completely submerged; bring to a boil. Reduce heat and simmer, covered, for 20 minutes to develop flavors. Remove and discard lemongrass.

3. Drain noodles and add to soup along with sliced green onion tops, mushrooms, shrimp and lime juice. When hot and shrimp (if previously uncooked) are bright pink, stir in coconut milk. Taste and adjust seasoning as needed. Heat until hot, but do not boil. Ladle into warmed soup bowls; garnish with several whole coriander leaves.

Fresh Seafood Chowder

Finding really fresh fish and seafood can be a frustrating experience when you live far from the sea. But if you choose carefully you can still create a delicious and flavorful chowder using frozen ingredients. Thaw the fish slowly in the refrigerator and remove when partially defrosted; in this state, fish is easier to cut into neat chunks.

4	slices bacon	4
1	onion, finely chopped	1
1	large carrot, diced	1
1	stalk celery, diced	1
1/4 cup	all-purpose flour	50 mL
2 cups	fish or chicken stock, cooled or water	500 mL
1	large potato, peeled and diced	1
1/4 tsp	dried savory	1 mL
1	large sprig fresh thyme	1
1	bay leaf	1
2 lbs	frozen boneless fish fillets (such as sole, haddock or bluefish), defrosted and cut into 1-inch (2.5 cm) chunks	1 kg
1 lb	frozen scallops, defrosted	500 g
1 lb	frozen peeled shrimp, uncooked or cooked, defrosted	500 g
2 cups	whole milk	500 mL
1/4 cup	finely chopped parsley or thinly sliced green onions	50 mL
1/4 tsp	black pepper	1 mL

1. In a large saucepan over medium heat, sauté bacon until lightly browned. Add onion, carrot and celery; cook for 5 minutes or until onion is softened. Sprinkle with flour; stir until absorbed. Slide pan off heat. Add stock a little at a time (to avoid lumps), stirring after each addition until smooth.

2. Return saucepan to heat. Add potato, savory, thyme and bay leaf; bring to a boil. Reduce heat and simmer, covered, for 20 minutes or until potatoes are tender. Increase heat to medium. Add fish, scallops and shrimp; cook, covered, for 5 minutes or until fish is opaque and shrimp are pink or hot. Gently stir in milk, half of the parsley and pepper. Heat until hot. Taste and adjust seasoning as needed. Ladle into warmed soup bowls; garnish with remaining parsley.

Broccoli and Cheese Chowder

Some years ago, former U.S. president George Bush made the news by declaring his dislike for broccoli. But here's a soup that even he might like. In this recipe we've created an unusual variation on the old standard — stirring broccoli florets and grated carrot into a thick purée of vegetables.

1	bunch broccoli	1
2 tbsp	butter or canola oil	25 mL
1	Spanish or other sweet onion, diced	1
2	stalks celery, sliced	2
2	cloves garlic, minced	2
1/4 cup	all-purpose flour	50 mL
6 cups	chicken stock	1.5 L
1/4 tsp	dried leaf thyme	1 mL
1	bay leaf	1
2	large carrots, grated	2
2 cups	whole milk	500 mL
1/2 tsp	salt	2 mL
1/4 tsp	freshly ground black pepper	1 mL
1 cup	grated Cheddar cheese	250 mL

1. Cut broccoli tops into very small florets. Peel remaining thick stems; cut into chunks. In a large saucepan, melt butter over medium heat. Stir in onion, celery and garlic; cook for 5 minutes or until softened. Sprinkle with flour; stir until absorbed. Slide pan off heat. Add stock, a little at a time (to avoid lumps), stirring after each addition until smooth.

2. Return saucepan to heat. Add broccoli stems, thyme and bay leaf; bring to a boil. Reduce heat and simmer, covered and stirring occasionally, for 15 minutes or until vegetables are tender. Remove bay leaf. Purée in a blender or food processor; return to saucepan.

3. Heat soup until hot; stir in grated carrots. Reduce heat and simmer, covered, for 10 minutes. Stir in broccoli florets; simmer for 5 minutes. Stir in milk, salt and pepper. Heat until hot. Taste and adjust seasoning as needed. Ladle into heated soup bowls; garnish with a generous sprinkle of grated Cheddar.

Creamy Corn 'n' Cheddar Chowder

One of the world's greatest cheeses, Cheddar was developed centuries ago in the English town of the same name. In Britain and Canada, this cows' milk cheese is left to develop for 2 to 5 years or more, its flavor becoming sharper with age. U.S. Cheddars usually age for just a few months. In this recipe, old-world Cheddar meets new-world corn in a smooth, rich chowder that pleases young kids and ravenous teens as well as sophisticated grown-ups.

2 tbsp	butter	25 mL
1	onion, diced	1
1	clove garlic, minced	1
1 tsp	Dijon mustard	5 mL
½ tsp	paprika	2 mL
¼ cup	all-purpose flour	50 mL
3 cups	chicken stock	750 mL
3 or 4	Yukon Gold or white potatoes, peeled and diced	3 or 4
½ tsp	salt	2 mL
1 ½ cups	corn kernels, fresh or frozen, thawed and drained	375 mL
2 cups	whole milk or half-and-half (10%) cream	500 mL
¼ cup	sliced green onions	50 mL
2 cups	grated old Cheddar cheese (about 8 oz/250 g)	500 mL

1. In a large saucepan, melt butter over medium heat. Stir in onion, garlic, mustard and paprika; cook for 5 minutes or until softened. Sprinkle with flour; stir until absorbed. Slide pan off heat. Add stock a little at a time (to avoid lumps), stirring after each addition until smooth.

2. Return saucepan to heat. Add potatoes and salt; bring to a boil. Reduce heat and simmer, covered and stirring occasionally, for 10 to 15 minutes or until potatoes are tender. Add corn, milk and green onions; heat until hot, but do not boil. Add half of the cheese, stirring briefly until melted. (Over-stirring can make cheese stringy.) Ladle into warmed soup bowls; serve sprinkled with remaining cheese. Provide a pepper grinder to pass at the table.

Marilyn's Note

My husband Michael is a Cheddar connoisseur. He especially loves old Cheddar from Ontario's Wilton Cheese Factory for its outstanding taste and smooth texture.

When temperatures drop and the dark days of winter settle in, there's nothing more soothing than a bowl of hearty soup. We often double recipes so we can pop some in the freezer for later. Most of our recipes are so rib-sticking and warming they'd make a delicious lunch or dinner meal, especially if accompanied by fresh warm chunky bread, a salad and some cheese and fruit for dessert. Our mouths are watering just thinking about it!

Hearty

Julentini Soup. 108

Curried Squash and Cider Soup 110

Butternut Squash Soup with Toasted Seeds 111

Fiery Fall Pumpkin Soup with Shrimp 112

Celeriac Potato Soup with Julienne. 114

Creamy Carrot Soup with Peanut Sauce Drizzle 115

Fennel Soup with Cambozola 116

Toasted Hazelnut Cremini Mushroom Soup. 117

Creamy Celery and Celeriac Soup. 118

Cream of Jerusalem Artichoke Soup
    with Hot Pepper Rouille 119

Lentil Dal Soup 120

Italian Lentil Soup with Sausage. 121

Mexican Chili Bean and Corn Soup 122

White Bean Soup with Barley 123

Brazilian Black Bean Soup. 124

Prosciutto and Pea Soup 125

Julentini Soup

This recipe comes to us via Barbara Podhorodeski, from her mother Judy Jones, and her mother's neighbor Judy Sakundiak Stevenson. It dates back to the early 1980s, when the Jones and Stevenson families started to grow lentils — then a relatively unknown crop — on their farms in Saskatchewan. To build awareness among other farmers, they held "mini field days," when participants learned how lentils were grown and used by consumers. To finish off, the two Judys served up bowls of this hearty lentil soup, which became known as Ju-lenti-ni Soup.

Tips

Chicken bouillon comes in cubes, rectangles and powders. A cube or 1 tsp (5 mL) powder usually flavors about 1 cup (250 mL) of water. Our favorite bouillon is Knorr powder and rectangles (each rectangle flavors 2 cups/500 mL of water).

For a vegetarian version of this soup, omit the ham bone and simmering time and use vegetable bouillon cubes to create the stock.

1	ham bone	1
12 cups	cold water	3 L
1	bay leaf	1
2 cups	brown or green lentils, picked over and washed	500 mL
2	large potatoes, peeled and diced	2
1	carrot, sliced	1
1	large onion, chopped	1
2½ cups	canned diced tomatoes, including juice	625 mL
1	clove garlic, minced	1
¼ tsp	black pepper	1 mL
1 tbsp	dried parsley (or ¼ cup/ 50 mL finely chopped fresh)	15 mL
½ tsp	dried oregano	2 mL
½ tsp	dried basil (or 2 tbsp/25 mL finely chopped fresh)	2 mL
2	chicken bouillon cubes or 2 tsp (10 mL) chicken bouillon powder (optional)	2
1 to 2 cups	grated mozzarella cheese	250 to 500 mL

1. In a large pot, combine ham bone, water and bay leaf; bring to a boil, skimming off and discarding any foam that rises to the surface. Reduce heat and simmer, partially covered, for 1 hour.

2. Increase heat; add lentils, potatoes, carrot, onion, tomatoes (with juice), garlic, pepper, dried parsley, dried oregano and dried basil. Taste and, if salty enough, omit bouillon cubes, otherwise stir in cubes. Bring to a boil; reduce heat. Simmer, covered, for 30 minutes or until thick; remove ham bone. Chop any ham that remains clinging to the bone and add it to the soup; discard bone. If using fresh herbs, add them now. Ladle into warmed soup bowls; garnish with grated mozzarella cheese.

Curried Squash and Cider Soup

The essence of autumn, this easy-to-prepare soup contains two of our favorite ingredients: apple cider and squash. Curry powder and cumin give it a warm Indian hint while the yogurt cools it down.

1 tbsp	butter	15 mL
1	onion, very finely chopped	1
2	cloves garlic, minced	2
2 tsp	curry powder	10 mL
1/2 tsp	ground cumin	2 mL
2 tbsp	all-purpose flour	25 mL
4 to	unsweetened apple cider	1 to
5 cups	or apple juice	1.25 L
1	pkg (14 oz/400 g) frozen puréed squash or 2 cups (500 mL) cooked puréed squash (thick consistency)	1
1/2 tsp	salt	2 mL
1/8 tsp	cayenne	0.5 mL
1/2 cup	yogurt or sour cream	125 mL
1	green onion, thinly sliced	1
	Parsnip Crisps (see recipe, page 34)	

1. In a large saucepan, melt butter over medium heat. Add onion and garlic; cook for 5 minutes or until softened. Stir in curry and cumin; cook for 1 minute. Stir in flour; cook 1 minute. Slide pan off heat; gradually stir in 4 cups (1 L) of the cider.

2. Return saucepan to heat. Stir in squash, salt and cayenne; bring to a boil. Reduce heat and simmer, partially covered, for 10 minutes. If soup is too thick, thin with remaining cider. Taste and adjust seasonings as needed. Ladle into warmed soup bowls; garnish with a dollop of yogurt and a sprinkling of green onion. Serve accompanied with a basket of Parsnip Crisps to pass at the table.

Butternut Squash Soup with Toasted Seeds

Serves 8

*Most winter squashes —
including butternut,
Hubbard, acorn and
pepper varieties — work
well in puréed soups
and can be used
interchangeably.*

Tip

Don't throw out squash
or pumpkin seeds: make
a nibbler or soup topping
from them. Here's how:
wipe off all the pulp that
clings to the seeds, toss
them with a tiny amount
of canola or olive oil and
spread them out on a
baking pan. Lightly
sprinkle with salt and
pepper. Bake in a
preheated 350°F (180°C)
oven for 10 minutes,
stirring occasionally, or
until golden. Remove
from the pan as soon
as they are done, let
cool and store in an
air-tight container.

- *Preheat oven to 350°F (180°C)*

4 lbs	butternut or other winter squash, cut in half and seeded	2 kg
2 tbsp	butter	25 mL
4	leeks, white and light green parts only, sliced	4
2	large sprigs fresh thyme (or 1/2 tsp/2 mL dried)	2
5 cups	chicken stock or vegetable stock	1.25 L
1 tsp	salt	5 mL
1/2 tsp	black pepper	2 mL
1/2 cup	sour cream	125 mL
1/4 cup	toasted squash or pumpkin seeds (for technique, see tip, at left) Parmesan Shortbreads (see recipe, page 42)	50 mL

1. Place squash, cut-side down, on a baking sheet. Bake in preheated oven for 40 minutes or until tender. Set aside until cool enough to handle; scoop out cooked squash. Discard skins.

2. Meanwhile, in a large saucepan, melt butter over low heat. Add leeks and thyme; cook, stirring occasionally, for 30 to 35 minutes or until soft and lightly browned. Remove thyme sprigs. Stir in stock and cooked squash; bring to a boil. Reduce heat and simmer, partially covered, for 20 minutes.

3. In a blender or food processor, purée soup in batches and return to saucepan. Heat until hot; stir in salt and pepper. Taste and adjust seasonings as needed. Ladle into warmed soup bowls; garnish with a dollop of sour cream and a sprinkling of seeds. Serve accompanied with a plate of Parmesan Shortbreads to pass at the table.

Fiery Fall Pumpkin Soup with Shrimp

The pie pumpkin used here is much smaller than the huge jack-o'-lantern variety. Its flesh is a deeper orange and contains much less moisture. Various types of winter squash can be substituted for the pumpkin.

Tips

Fish sauce is very salty so be sure to wait until you have thoroughly stirred it in and tasted the soup before adding extra salt. Be sure to use coconut milk (found in the Asian-food section of supermarkets) — not sweetened coconut cream, which is used to make "girlie" cocktails (such as piña coladas) and is found in the drinks section.

When working with hot peppers, it's best to wear latex gloves or to rub your hands with vegetable oil before starting. Be careful not to put your hands to your face or eyes, otherwise you'll experience a burning sensation that is hard to quell.

1 tbsp	canola oil	15 mL
4	shallots, minced	4
2	cloves garlic, minced	2
3 cups	chicken stock	750 mL
2 cups	peeled, seeded and cubed pie pumpkin or squash	500 mL
1 tbsp	fish sauce	15 mL
1	tiny hot Thai red pepper, finely minced or 1/4 to 1/2 tsp (1 to 2 mL) crushed red pepper flakes	1
1	stalk lemongrass, bulb lightly crushed	1
1 cup	coconut milk	250 mL
1/2 tsp	lime juice	2 mL
4 oz	cooked salad shrimp	125 g
1/4 cup	coarsely chopped fresh coriander	50 mL

1. In a large saucepan, heat oil over medium heat. Add shallots and garlic; cook for 1 minute. Add stock, pumpkin, fish sauce, hot pepper and lemongrass; bring to a boil. Reduce heat and simmer, partially covered, for 10 to 15 minutes or until pumpkin is tender.

2. Remove lemongrass and discard. In a food processor or blender, purée soup in batches; return to saucepan. Stir in coconut milk and lime juice; heat until hot. Taste and add additional lime juice if desired. Stir in shrimp and half of the coriander. Ladle into warmed soup bowls; serve sprinkled with remaining coriander.

Celeriac Potato Soup with Julienne

Serves 8 to 10

Celeriac, or celery root, is one of the unsung heroes of the vegetable kingdom, overlooked by chefs and home cooks alike. It is, admittedly, not very attractive, looking a bit like a wrinkly, hairy white turnip.

Tips

Celeriac stores well and must be peeled (with a swivel peeler or paring knife) before using. It discolors quickly however, so if you must leave it for a few minutes before cooking, drop it into a bowl of cold water to which you've added 1 tbsp (15 mL) of lemon juice.

To "julienne" vegetables, cut them into small pieces the length and thickness of wooden match sticks.

1	large carrot	1
1	celeriac, peeled	1
2 tbsp	butter	25 mL
2	large leeks, white and light green parts only, sliced	2
4	shallots, peeled and sliced	4
4	baking potatoes, peeled and diced	4
8 cups	chicken stock	2 L
1	sprig fresh thyme (or ¼ tsp/1 mL dried)	1
1	bay leaf	1
½ tsp	salt	2 mL
¼ tsp	black pepper	1 mL
2	green onions, thinly sliced	2

1. Julienne carrot and half of celeriac (place celeriac into water acidified with lemon juice to prevent discoloring); set aside. In a large saucepan, melt butter over medium heat. Add leeks and shallots; cook for 5 minutes or until softened. Meanwhile, dice remaining celeriac; add to saucepan along with potatoes, stock, thyme and bay leaf. Bring to a boil; reduce heat and simmer, covered, for 20 minutes or until vegetables are soft. Discard thyme sprig and bay leaf.

2. In a blender or food processor, purée soup in batches; return to saucepan. Add drained julienne of celeriac and carrot; bring just to a boil over medium heat, stirring frequently. Reduce heat and simmer, partially covered and stirring frequently, for 10 minutes or until vegetables are tender. Stir in salt and pepper. Taste and adjust seasoning as needed. Ladle into warmed soup bowls; serve garnished with a sprinkling of green onions.

Creamy Carrot Soup with Peanut Sauce Drizzle

Librarian Maureen O'Connor serves dynamite soups that are always a little unusual. Here, she uses short-grain Arborio rice to thicken carrot soup, then adds an unexpected swirl of slightly sweet and spicy peanut sauce.

Tip

Short-grain rices such as Arborio (the essential ingredient for making classic risotto) contain a starch that produces a creamy texture. Long-grain rices, such as basmati or "converted" or "parboiled" varieties require less water for cooking; the grains stay separate and can be "fluffed." These do not thicken puréed soups as well as short-grain rices.

1 tbsp	butter	15 mL
1	onion, sliced	1
1	stalk celery, sliced	1
1	clove garlic, minced	1
4	medium carrots, sliced	4
2 cups	chicken stock or vegetable stock	500 mL
1/4 cup	Arborio or other short-grain rice	50 mL
1/2 tsp	salt	2 mL
1/4 tsp	black pepper	1 mL
1/2 cup	half-and-half (10%) cream or whole milk	125 mL
1/4 cup	peanut sauce (homemade or bottled)	50 mL
2 tbsp	finely chopped fresh parsley	25 mL

1. In a large saucepan, melt butter over medium heat. Add onion, celery and garlic; cook for 5 minutes or until softened. Stir in carrots, stock, and rice; bring to a boil. Reduce heat and simmer, partially covered, for 20 minutes or until carrots and rice are tender.

2. In a blender or food processor, purée soup in batches; return to saucepan. Heat until hot; stir in salt, pepper and cream. Taste and adjust seasoning as needed. Ladle into warmed soup bowls; garnish with a drizzle of peanut sauce and a sprinkling of parsley.

Fennel Soup with Cambozola

We love fennel for its crunchiness when raw and for the mild anise flavor it adds to cooked dishes — a flavor that works particularly well with creamy cheeses in a soup. Here we put chunks of the cheese in the bottom of each soup bowl before pouring in the hot soup, which only slightly melts the cheese; the result is that the cheese is not fully incorporated into the soup, also providing a surprise for guests when they reach the bottom of the bowl! Cambozola, a relatively recent entrant in the cheese market, combines mild Camembert and robust Gorgonzola, a classic blue cheese. In our minds, it's a brilliant marriage.

1 tbsp	butter	15 mL
1	onion, chopped	1
2	bulbs fennel, feathery green ends discarded, sliced	2
1	clove garlic, minced	1
1/4 cup	all-purpose flour	50 mL
3 cups	chicken stock or vegetable stock, cooled	750 mL
1/4 cup	dry white wine	50 mL
1 cup	whole milk	250 mL
1/2 tsp	salt	2 mL
1/4 tsp	black pepper	1 mL
4 oz	Cambozola or Gorgonzola cheese	125 g
2 tbsp	finely chopped fresh parsley	25 mL

1. In a large saucepan, melt butter over medium heat. Add onion, fennel and garlic; cook for 5 minutes or until softened. Stir in flour; cook for 1 minute. Slide pan off heat. Slowly stir in stock and wine. Bring to a boil. Reduce heat and simmer, partially covered, for 20 minutes or until fennel is tender.

2. In a blender or food processor, purée soup in batches; return to saucepan. Stir in milk, salt and pepper; heat until hot. Taste and adjust seasoning as needed. Divide cheese among warmed soup bowls; ladle in soup. Serve garnished with a sprinkling of parsley.

Toasted Hazelnut Cremini Mushroom Soup

Serves 4 to 6

Cremini mushrooms are also called brown mushrooms. But whatever you call them, they're especially flavorful and a great addition to soups. If you can't find any cremini for this soup, buy regular button mushrooms or use a mixture of several varieties.

Tip

Toasting the hazelnuts brings out their nutty flavor: Set the nuts in a single layer in a baking pan and pop into an oven preheated to 350°F (180°C); bake for 8 to 10 minutes or until lightly browned. Set aside to cool, then transfer the nuts to a kitchen towel. Rub the nuts with the towel until most of the papery skins fall off. (Step outside and shake towel to get rid of the clinging skins.) Chop nuts with a chef's knife or with a few quick pulses in a blender or food processor.

1 tbsp	butter	15 mL
1	onion, diced	1
1	clove garlic, minced	1
1 lb	cremini or other mushrooms, sliced	500 g
4 cups	chicken stock	1 L
1	sprig fresh thyme	1
1	bay leaf	1
1/2 cup	toasted hazelnuts (for technique, see tip, at left)	125 mL
1/2 tsp	salt	2 mL
1/4 tsp	black pepper	1 mL
2 tbsp	chopped fresh parsley	25 mL

1. In a large saucepan, heat butter over medium heat. Add onion and garlic; cook for 5 minutes or until softened. Add mushrooms, stock, thyme and bay leaf; bring to a boil. Reduce heat and simmer, partially covered and stirring occasionally, for 15 minutes. Remove thyme sprig and bay leaf.

2. Coarsely chop nuts; set one-third aside and add remainder to soup. In a blender or food processor, purée soup in batches until very smooth; return to saucepan. Heat until hot; stir in salt and pepper. Taste and adjust seasonings as needed. Ladle into warm soup bowls; serve garnished with a sprinkling of parsley and remaining chopped nuts.

Creamy Celery and Celeriac Soup

Serves 6 to 8

We like celeriac so much we've used it more than once as a starring ingredient in our soups (see also Celeriac Potato Soup with Julienne, *page 114). Here we've paired it with its above-ground counterpart, the common stalk celery. This is a very subtly flavored soup, which is sure to be a hit with your guests — and a challenge, as they try to identify the mystery ingredient.*

Tip

A blender produces the smoothest purées and works most efficiently when plenty of broth is added while blending. A food processor works best with less liquid, and the resulting purée will not be as silky as that from a blender. Hand blenders are a dandy timesaver since puréeing can be done right in the saucepan, although you may end up with a few chunks that escape the blades.

1 tbsp	butter	15 mL
1	onion, diced	1
1	large carrot, diced	1
2	stalks celery, diced	2
1	celeriac, peeled and diced	1
6 cups	chicken stock	1.5 L
½ tsp	chopped fresh tarragon (or ¼ tsp/1 mL dried)	2 mL
1	bay leaf	1
2 cups	whole milk	500 mL
½ tsp	salt	2 mL
¼ tsp	black pepper	1 mL
2 tbsp	chopped fresh parsley	25 mL

1. In a large saucepan, melt butter over medium heat. Add onion, carrot, celery and celeriac; cook, stirring occasionally, for 10 minutes or until softened. Add stock, tarragon and bay leaf; bring to a boil. Reduce heat and simmer, partially covered, for 20 minutes or until vegetables are tender. Discard bay leaf.

2. In a blender or food processor, purée soup in batches; return to saucepan. Stir in milk, salt and pepper. Taste and adjust seasoning as needed. Heat until hot, but do not allow to boil. Ladle into warmed soup bowls; serve garnished with a sprinkling of parsley.

Cream of Jerusalem Artichoke Soup with Hot Pepper Rouille

Serves 6

2 lbs	Jerusalem artichokes	1 kg
2 tbsp	butter	25 mL
1	onion, diced	1
2½ cups	chicken stock	625 mL
1¼ cups	whole milk	300 mL
½ cup	whipping (35%) cream	125 mL
½ tsp	salt	2 mL
¼ tsp	black pepper	1 mL
	Hot Pepper Rouille (see recipe, page 39)	

1. Peel artichokes under cold running water. As each tuber is peeled, place it in a bowl of cold water acidified with 1 tbsp (15 mL) lemon juice. (This will prevent discoloring.) Slice tubers and return to water.

2. In a large saucepan, melt butter over medium heat. Add onion and well-drained artichoke slices; cook, covered and stirring occasionally, for 10 minutes. Add stock and milk; simmer for 35 minutes or until vegetables are tender. Do not allow to boil.

3. In a food processor or blender, purée soup in batches; return to saucepan. Heat until hot; stir in cream, salt and pepper. Taste and adjust seasoning as needed. Ladle into warmed soup bowls; garnish with a dollop of Hot Pepper Rouille.

Joan's Note

I was first served this soup in England and liked it so much that I returned to Canada with the recipe and, in the following spring, innocently planted a row of Jerusalem artichoke tubers in my garden. By the end of that summer, much to my horror, the plants had grown more than 8 feet tall, and had spread their knobby roots throughout my entire garden. It was years before I was able to rid the garden of these monsters. Having learned my lesson, I now buy them in the supermarket, where they are sometimes packaged as "sunchokes." They're delicious raw in salads, cooked in gratins or puréed in soups — and, being rich in Vitamin C and carbohydrates, they're good for you too.

Lentil Dal Soup

Serves 4 to 6

Tips

By substituting vegetable stock for chicken stock, you will have a vegetarian soup that tastes just as good.

Lentils have been staple fare in many hot-weather countries for centuries. They are highly prized for their nutritional value and are rich in protein. Lentils are one of the few legumes that do not have to be soaked before cooking — split peas, both green and yellow, being another.

1 tbsp	butter	15 mL
1	onion, diced	1
1	clove garlic, minced	1
1½ tsp	curry powder	7 mL
½ tsp	ground cumin	2 mL
1	large carrot, diced	1
1	stalk celery, diced	1
1 cup	red lentils	250 mL
4 cups	chicken stock or vegetable stock	1 L
¼ cup	finely chopped fresh parsley	50 mL
1 tbsp	lemon juice	15 mL
½ tsp	salt	5 mL
¼ tsp	black pepper	1 mL
	Naan or whole-wheat pita bread	

1. In a large saucepan, melt butter over medium heat. Add onion and garlic; cook, stirring occasionally, for 5 minutes or until softened. Stir in curry powder and cumin; cook for 2 minutes. Add carrot, celery, lentils and chicken stock; bring to a boil. Reduce heat and simmer, partially covered and stirring occasionally, for 15 to 20 minutes or until soup has thickened.

2. Stir in half of the parsley, lemon juice, salt and pepper. Taste and adjust seasoning as needed. Ladle into warmed soup bowls; garnish with a sprinkling of remaining parsley. Serve with warm naan or whole-wheat pita bread.

Marilyn's Note

One of the pleasures of an Indian meal is a side dish of dal. In fact, I like it so much that I added some extra stock and veggies to come up with this really flavorful soup. Sometimes I grind my own curry powder — using a combination of turmeric, coriander, cayenne pepper and cumin seed — so that I know exactly how hot it will be.

Italian Lentil Soup with Sausage

Serves 4 to 6

When shopping for sausage, remember that it can vary tremendously in quality. Skillful sausage makers keep pork very cold when coarsely grinding the meat, so the sausages have a clear definition between meat, spices and a bit of necessary white fat. The resulting texture is far superior to most "supermarket" varieties, which have a consistency closer to that of breakfast sausage.

Tips

Like most sausages, Italian sausage contains a fair amount of fat and salt, so there's no need to add any extra when making this soup.

Remember — the hotter the sausage, the hotter the soup! If your soup isn't as hot as you'd like, add a shot of hot pepper sauce or a few crushed red pepper flakes towards the end of the cooking time.

For a light supper, serve this soup with Italian bread and tossed green salad.

2	Italian sausages, casings removed, crumbled	2
1	onion, diced	1
1	clove garlic, minced	1
1	large potato, peeled and diced	1
1	carrot, diced	1
1	stalk celery, diced	1
1/2 cup	brown or green lentils	125 mL
2 cups	canned diced tomatoes, including juice or 2 large ripe tomatoes, seeded and diced	500 mL
4 to 5 cups	unsalted chicken, beef or vegetable stock or water	1 to 1.25 L
1/4 tsp	black pepper	1 mL
2 tbsp	finely chopped fresh parsley	25 mL

1. In a large saucepan over medium heat, cook sausage, stirring often to break up the meat, for 10 minutes or until lightly browned. Drain and discard any fat. Add onion and garlic; cook for 5 minutes or until softened. Add potato, carrot, celery, lentils, tomatoes (with juice) and 4 cups (1 L) stock; bring to a boil. Reduce heat and simmer, partially covered and stirring frequently, for 20 minutes or until lentils are cooked.

2. Stir in pepper and parsley. If soup is very thick, thin by adding remaining stock. Taste and adjust seasonings as needed. Ladle into warm soup bowls.

Mexican Chili Bean and Corn Soup

This spicy robust soup is a chili-head's delight. While true heat-seekers will want to splash in some hot pepper sauce, the spice hit in every spoonful of this soup will certainly be enough for most people. It's perfect served with a big basket of warmed tortilla chips.

1 tbsp	canola oil	15 mL
1	onion, diced	1
1	clove garlic, minced	1
2 tbsp	chili powder	25 mL
1 tsp	ground cumin	5 mL
2 cups	diced canned tomatoes, with juice or 2 large tomatoes, cut into chunks	500 mL
2 cups	water	500 mL
1	can (15 1/2 oz/439 g or 19 oz/540 mL) red kidney or romano beans, drained but not rinsed	1
1	small green bell pepper, seeded and diced	1
1	jalapeño pepper, seeded and minced or 2 tbsp (25 mL) canned diced green chilies	1
1/8 tsp	cayenne	0.5 mL
1 cup	corn kernels, fresh (or frozen, thawed and drained)	250 mL
1/4 cup	chopped fresh coriander or parsley	50 mL
1/2 tsp	salt	2 mL

1. In a large saucepan, heat oil over medium heat. Add onion and garlic; cook for 5 minutes or until softened. Stir in chili powder and cumin; cook for 1 minute. Add tomatoes (with juice), water, beans, green pepper, jalapeño pepper and cayenne; bring to a boil. Reduce heat and simmer, partially covered and stirring frequently, for 20 minutes or until vegetables are soft. Stir in corn, coriander and salt; heat until hot. Taste and adjust seasoning as needed. Ladle into warmed soup bowls.

White Bean Soup with Barley

Here's the perfect soup to serve to a crowd who've just come in from an invigorating day in the cold outdoors. It's a soup-maker's dream: it can be made several days ahead, it freezes beautifully and, like chili, tastes even better when reheated.

Tip

We like to soak beans overnight, but if you're short on time, try this quick-soak method: Generously cover beans with water; bring to a boil. Remove from heat and let sit for 1 hour; drain. If you use vegetable stock as your liquid, this makes a dandy vegetarian soup.

1 1/2 cups	white beans (great Northern, navy or other variety)	375 mL
1 tbsp	olive oil or canola oil	15 mL
1	large onion, diced	1
2	cloves garlic, minced	2
3	carrots, diced	3
3	stalks celery, diced	3
2	red bell peppers, seeded and diced	2
1/2 cup	pot or pearl barley	125 mL
1	can (28 oz/796 mL) diced tomatoes, including juice	1
8 cups	chicken or vegetable stock or water	2 L
1/2 tsp	dried leaf thyme	2 mL
2	bay leaves	2
1/2 tsp	black pepper	2 mL
1/4 tsp	salt	1 mL
1/2 cup	chopped fresh parsley	125 mL
	Whole-wheat or corn bread	

1. Place beans in a large bowl. Pick over beans, discarding any small stones you find. Add sufficient cold water to cover beans by several inches (to allow for expansion). Let sit overnight at room temperature or in the refrigerator; drain just before using.

2. In a large pot, heat oil over medium heat. Add onion and garlic; cook for 5 minutes or until softened. Add drained beans, carrots, celery, bell peppers, barley, tomatoes (with juice), stock, thyme and bay leaves; bring to a boil. Reduce heat and simmer, covered, for 2 hours or until beans are tender. Remove bay leaves; stir in black pepper, salt and half of the parsley. Taste and adjust seasonings as needed. Ladle into warmed bowls; garnish with a sprinkling of remaining parsley. Serve with thick slices of whole-wheat or corn bread.

Brazilian Black Bean Soup

Serves 6

There's nothing subtle about the flavor of black beans; like coriander, they have a flavor you'll either love or hate. While there is no denying that home-cooked black beans are far superior to those from a can, the convenience of the latter choice often wins out.

Tips

If you've got the energy and freezer space, try this method for preparing black and other beans in bulk: soak a large quantity of beans overnight, then gently boil them on the following day until just tender. (The consistency should be like al dente pasta.) Drain, measure into resealable freezer bags and remove as much air as possible before sealing. They'll keep for months in the freezer; when ready to use, just toss 'em into soup while still frozen.

Hot cornmeal muffins make a delicious accompaniment to this soup.

1 tbsp	canola oil	15 mL
1	onion, diced	1
1	clove garlic, minced	1
1	red bell pepper, seeded and diced	1
1	stalk celery, diced	1
2 tbsp	all-purpose flour	25 mL
4 cups	chicken or ham stock, cooled or water	1 L
2 cups	canned diced tomatoes, with juice or 2 large tomatoes, cut into chunks	500 mL
1	can (15½ oz/439 g or 19 oz/540 mL) black beans, drained but not rinsed	1
¼ tsp	dried leaf thyme	1 mL
½ tsp	salt (omit if using ham stock)	2 mL
¼ tsp	black pepper	1 mL
¼ tsp	hot pepper sauce	1 mL
¼ cup	chopped fresh coriander or parsley	50 mL

1. In a large saucepan, heat oil over medium heat. Add onion and garlic; cook for 5 minutes or until softened. Stir in bell pepper and celery; sprinkle with flour. Stir until absorbed; cook for 1 minute. Slide pan off heat. Slowly stir in stock. Return to heat; add tomatoes (with juice), beans and thyme; bring to a boil. Reduce heat and simmer, partially covered and stirring occasionally, for 30 minutes or until vegetables are soft.

2. Stir in salt, black pepper, hot pepper sauce and half of the coriander. Taste and adjust seasonings as needed. Ladle into warm bowls; garnish with a sprinkling of remaining coriander.

Prosciutto and Pea Soup

Rebeka Moscarello, a whiz in the kitchen, puts an Italian spin on traditional pea soup by using the bone from a prosciutto end in place of one from a smoked ham. Prosciutto crudo is raw salted ham that is cured for months under special conditions, much like Parmigiano-Reggiano cheese. A delicacy originating from the Italian province of Parma, this ham has a unique flavor and texture. It is available in Italian markets, delicatessens and sliced meat departments in many supermarkets. When sliced paper-thin from the wide portion of the ham, prosciutto is very expensive; but the prosciutto end, which is not suitable for slicing, is much more reasonably priced. Prosciutto ends are often not displayed, so you may have to ask for them at the deli counter.

1	bone from prosciutto end	1
1 lb	green split peas (about 2 cups/500 mL)	500 g
2	large carrots, cut into chunks	2
1	large onion	1
6 to 7 cups	water	1.5 to 1.75 L
½ tsp	lemon juice	2 mL
	Parsley Butter Coins (see recipe, page 41)	

1. In a small saucepan, generously cover prosciutto with cold water; bring to a boil. Remove from heat; drain. Rinse bone under lukewarm running water. If the bone and meat are tied with string, remove and discard it.

2. In a bowl cover peas with cold water and stir gently. When water turns murky, drain the peas through a strainer, then return to the bowl. Add more water, stir and drain again. Repeat process until the water no longer grows cloudy. Remove outer brown skin from onion. Cut off and discard root end; leave tapered end intact.

3. In a large pot, combine parboiled bone, rinsed peas, carrots and whole onion. Add 6 cups (1.5 L) water; bring to a boil. Reduce heat and simmer, partially covered and stirring frequently, for 2 to 3 hours or until peas are soft and meat falls from the bone. Add remaining water if needed.

4. Remove bone. If desired, mash carrots into soup. Taste and adjust seasoning as needed. If desired, add more lemon juice. Ladle into warmed soup bowls; serve garnished with a Parsley Butter Coin.

When company comes, we all like to please our guests by making dishes that take a little extra effort. Most of the soups we have included in this chapter can be started a day ahead (or early in the day) of your dinner party and finished off at the end. We'll bet you are bombarded with recipe requests.

Fancies

Chicken Soup with Celestine Threads 128

Cream of Watercress Soup with Sea Scallops 129

Mushroom Soup with Puff Pastry Dome 130

Seeing-Double Soup 132

Roasted Sweet Potato Soup
  with Ginger Orange Crème Fraîche 134

Fresh Clam and Fall Vegetable Soup 136

Roasted Tomato Bisque with Sea Salt Wedges 138

Garlicky Chunky Chicken Soup 139

Moroccan Cumin Chicken Soup 140

Chili Lime Chicken Soup 141

Sole Velouté with Diced Vegetables 142

Chicken Soup with Celestine Threads

Serves 4 to 6

Use your best clear chicken stock (preferably homemade) to create this very light but elegant soup. It's a perfect starter for a rich meal.

Tip

While this soup is prepared best just before serving, you can get all the ingredients sliced and shredded in advance so they are ready to pop into the pot.

6 cups	chicken stock	1.5 L
2 tbsp	dry white wine	25 mL
2	skinless boneless chicken breasts, cut into 1/2-inch (1 cm) chunks	2
1 cup	shredded fresh Swiss chard or spinach or sliced snow peas	250 mL
1/2 tsp	salt	2 mL
1/4 tsp	black pepper	1 mL
6	Celestine Crêpes, cut into shreds (see recipe, page 37)	6

1. In a large saucepan, bring stock and white wine to a boil. Pat chicken dry with paper towels. One piece at a time, drop chicken into boiling stock. Simmer, uncovered, for 5 minutes. Stir in chard, salt and pepper. Taste and adjust seasonings as needed. Place crêpe threads in bottom of warmed soup bowls; ladle in soup. Serve immediately.

White Bean Soup with Barley • *page 123*

Overleaf:
New Orleans Gumbo • *page 178*

Cream of Watercress Soup with Sea Scallops

The success of this recipe depends on slicing scallops thinly enough that the heat of the soup alone is sufficient to cook them to tender and juicy perfection. That means using sea scallops, which are larger (and costlier) than bay scallops.

Tips

Scallops are often sold with a small piece of white muscle stuck to the side. This tissue is tough and inedible, so be sure to remove and discard it.

Pick out a few small perfect watercress sprigs and save them as a garnish for the soup.

1 tbsp	butter	15 mL
2	bunches watercress, coarse stems removed, washed thoroughly	2
2	small shallots, minced	2
1 ½ cups	chicken stock	375 mL
⅛ tsp	cayenne pepper	0.5 mL
Half	pkg (10 oz/284 g) spinach, coarse stems removed, washed thoroughly	Half
12	sea scallops (about 5 oz/140 g)	12
1 cup	whipping (35%) cream	250 mL
½ tsp	salt	2 mL

1. In a large saucepan, melt butter over medium heat. Add watercress leaves and shallots; cook for 5 minutes or until wilted. Add stock and cayenne; bring to a boil. Reduce heat and simmer, covered, for 15 minutes. Add spinach leaves; simmer for 5 minutes.

2. Meanwhile, with a sharp knife, cut scallops crosswise into very thin slices, being sure to keep their round shape; return to refrigerator. When soup mixture is cooked, purée in a blender or food processor. For smoothest texture, force purée through a sieve back into saucepan; discard remaining solids. Stir in cream and salt. Taste and adjust seasoning as needed.

3. When ready to serve, heat soup until very hot, but not boiling. Divide sliced raw scallops among warmed bowls; ladle soup over top. (The heat from the soup will cook the scallops.) Serve immediately.

Mushroom Soup with
Puff Pastry Dome • page 130

Mushroom Soup with Puff Pastry Dome

Serves 6

Imagine serving your guests bowls of fragrant mushroom soup capped by domes of golden puff pastry. You can almost hear the gasps of surprise!
For an elegant presentation, place bowls on underplates that are lined with large linen napkins folded in quarters.

Tip

You'll not want to be fiddling with this soup when your guests arrive, so make the mushroom and vegetable stock early in the day (or the day before) and refrigerate. Assemble the soups with their puff pastry domes in the late afternoon and chill. Just make sure that when you bake the soups in the oven, the liquid gets hot. If the pastry domes seem to be browning too quickly, cover each loosely with a piece of aluminum foil and continue baking.

- Preheat oven to 400°F (200°C)
- Six ovenproof soup bowls, each about 4 inches (10 cm) wide at top

1 lb	mixed mushrooms (such as shiitake, cremini, oyster, chanterelle and portobello)	500 g
6 cups	chicken stock	1.5 L
8 oz	button mushrooms, sliced	250 g
2 tbsp	butter	25 mL
1	leek, white and light green parts only, sliced	1
1	carrot, julienned or finely diced	1
1	stalk celery, julienned or finely diced	1
½ tsp	salt	2 mL
¼ tsp	black pepper	1 mL
1	pkg (14 oz/397 g) frozen puff pastry, defrosted overnight in refrigerator	1
1	egg, lightly beaten	1

1. Wipe mixed mushrooms with a paper towel. Trim mixed mushrooms, reserving trimmings and stems; slice mushrooms caps thinly and set aside. In a large saucepan, combine reserved trimmings and stems with stock and button mushrooms; bring to a boil. Reduce heat and simmer, covered, for 20 minutes. Place a cheesecloth-lined sieve over a bowl; strain broth, discarding solids. Return broth to saucepan and set aside.

2. In a large skillet, melt butter over medium-high heat. Add leek, carrot, celery and sliced mixed mushrooms; sauté, stirring frequently, for 1 to 2 minutes or until just hot. Add to broth in saucepan; bring to a boil. Reduce heat and simmer for 5 minutes. Stir in salt and pepper. Taste and adjust seasonings as needed.

3. *Puff pastry lids:* Roll out pastry thinly (to about ⅛ inch/3 mm thick). Using an inverted soup bowl as a guide, cut 6 circles of pastry, each 1½ inches (4 cm) larger in diameter than the bowl.

4. Ladle soup into bowls until three-quarters full. Brush egg over rim and ½ inch (1 cm) down outer side of bowl; brush both sides of pastry. Without stretching, place circles on top of bowls; press firmly to bowl rims and sides. Set bowls on a baking sheet; refrigerate uncovered for 20 minutes — or, lightly covered, for up to half a day.

5. About half an hour before serving, transfer bowls on baking sheet directly from refrigerator to preheated oven; bake for 10 minutes. Reduce heat to 375°F (190°C); bake for an additional 15 to 20 minutes or until pastry is nicely browned. Serve immediately.

Seeing-Double Soup

Two different soups of contrasting colors and flavors marry in one bowl for a spectacular presentation. Both can be made a day ahead and refrigerated. Reheat them in separate saucepans over low heat or in the tops of double boilers set over simmering water, stirring frequently.

SQUASH SOUP

1 tbsp	butter	15 mL
1	leek, white and light green parts only, sliced	1
1	onion, sliced	1
4	stalks celery, sliced	4
1	clove garlic, minced	1
4 cups	chicken stock	1 L
2	medium butternut squash, peeled, seeded and cubed	2
1/2 tsp	salt	2 mL
1/8 tsp	cayenne pepper	0.5 mL
1/2 cup	half-and-half (10%) cream	125 mL

LEEK SOUP

1 tbsp	butter	15 mL
2	leeks, white and light green parts only, sliced	2
4	stalks celery, sliced	4
1	large potato, peeled and sliced	1
1	bulb fennel, sliced (green fronds discarded)	1
1	clove garlic, minced	1
4 cups	chicken stock	1 L
1/4 cup	finely chopped fresh parsley	50 mL
1 tsp	lemon juice	5 mL
1/2 tsp	salt	2 mL
1/4 tsp	hot pepper sauce	1 mL
1/2 cup	half-and-half (10%) cream	125 mL

1. Use two large saucepans to make soups simultaneously. To make squash soup, melt butter over medium heat. Add leek, onion, celery and garlic; cook for 8 minutes or until softened. Add stock, squash and cayenne; bring to a boil. Reduce heat and simmer, covered, for 35 minutes or until vegetables are very soft.

2. To make leek soup, melt butter over medium heat. Add leeks, celery, potato, fennel and garlic; cook for 8 to 10 minutes or until softened. Add stock; bring to a boil. Reduce heat and simmer, covered, for 30 minutes or until vegetables are very soft.

3. In a blender or food processor, purée leek soup in batches. Stir in parsley, lemon juice, salt, hot pepper sauce and, if serving right away, cream. Return to saucepan over low heat. Without cleaning blender or food processor, purée squash soup. Stir in salt, cayenne and, if serving right away, cream; return to separate saucepan over low heat. Taste each soup and adjust seasonings as needed; heat until hot.

4. To serve, use two measuring cups to simultaneously pour soups into warmed bowls; soups should evenly meet in center of bowl. Using a skewer, swirl soups slightly into each other.

Roasted Sweet Potato Soup with Ginger Orange Crème Fraîche

Ginger and sweet potatoes are natural partners — each enhancing the flavor of the other. Here's a soup that can be prepared a day ahead, chilled, and then reheated in the top of a double boiler set over simmering water or in a saucepan over low heat. Stir the soup from time to time to distribute liquid evenly while heating.

Tip

For a crunchy and flavorful alternative to the parsley or green-onion garnish, try sprinkling the soup with toasted, coarsely chopped pecans.

- *Preheat oven to 400°F (200°C)*

1 cup	Crème Fraîche (see recipe, page 40) or sour cream	250 mL
1 tsp	finely grated ginger root	5 mL
1 tsp	finely grated orange zest	5 mL
3½ lbs	sweet potatoes, peeled and cut into small chunks	1.75 kg
¼ cup	melted butter	50 mL
1 tbsp	brown sugar	15 mL
1 tbsp	butter	15 mL
2 or 3	leeks, white and light green parts only, sliced	2 or 3
2	stalks celery, sliced	2
10 to 12 cups	chicken stock	2.5 to 3 L
1 cup	orange juice	250 mL
½ tsp	salt	2 mL
¼ tsp	black pepper	1 mL
¼ cup	finely chopped fresh parsley or thinly sliced green onions	50 mL

1. In a bowl stir together Crème Fraîche, ginger and orange zest. Cover and refrigerate. In another bowl, toss sweet potato cubes with ¼ cup (50 mL) melted butter and brown sugar. Spread in a single layer on a large baking sheet. Roast on top rack of preheated oven, stirring occasionally, for 30 minutes or until lightly browned.

2. In a large saucepan, melt 1 tbsp (15 mL) butter over medium heat. Add leeks and celery; cook for 8 to 10 minutes or until softened. Add 10 cups (2.5 L) stock, orange juice and roasted sweet potatoes; bring to a boil, stirring frequently. Reduce heat and simmer, partially covered, for 20 minutes. In a blender or food processor, purée in batches; return to pot. Add salt, black pepper and additional stock as required to thin soup to desired consistency; heat until hot. Taste and adjust seasonings as needed. Ladle into warmed bowls; add a dollop of Crème Fraîche. Using a skewer, swirl edges of Crème Fraîche slightly into surrounding soup; serve garnished with a sprinkling of parsley.

Fresh Clam and Fall Vegetable Soup

Fresh clams are one of the greatest culinary treasures of the sea. And for this recipe, at least, nothing else will really do. In fact, without fresh clams, you should forget about this soup and make something else. But if you do have fresh clams available, you're in for a treat. Not only is this soup delicious, but it's easy to make ahead of time, requiring only the final addition of cream and an egg yolk whisked into the tureen. To prepare ahead, cover and chill the clams and the broth separately, then reheat in the top of a double boiler, covered and set over a pot of simmering water.

Tip

Mussels can be used instead of clams (if you must!); in this case, reduce cooking time to 8 minutes. For either type of shellfish, be sure to discard any shells that do not open after cooking.

1 cup	water	250 mL
2	sprigs fresh parsley	2
1	sprig fresh thyme	1
1	shallot, minced	1
4 lbs	clams, scrubbed	2 kg
2 tbsp	butter	25 mL
1	large leek, white and light green parts only, thinly sliced	1
1	large carrot, thinly sliced	1
2	stalks celery, thinly sliced	2
3 tbsp	all-purpose flour	45 mL
3 cups	water or fish stock	750 mL
1	bulb fennel, sliced (green fronds discarded)	1
1/4 tsp	salt	1 mL
1/4 tsp	black pepper	1 mL
2 tbsp	chopped fresh parsley	25 mL
1/2 cup	whipping (35%) cream	125 mL
1	egg yolk	1
1	lemon, cut into wedges	1

1. In a large pot, combine water, parsley, thyme and shallot; bring to a boil. Add clams and tightly cover. Reduce heat slightly and boil gently for 10 to 15 minutes or until clams open. (Discard any that remain closed.) Remove clams from liquid. Place a cheesecloth-lined sieve over a bowl; strain broth. Working over the sieve, remove clam meat from shells; cover and refrigerate. Discard shells, first ensuring that any accumulated liquid strains back into broth. Set aside.

2. In a large saucepan, melt butter over medium heat. Add leek, carrot and celery; cook, stirring frequently, for 10 minutes or until softened. Sprinkle in flour; stir until absorbed. Slide pan off heat; gradually stir in water. Stir in reserved clam broth and fennel. Return to heat; bring to a boil, stirring frequently. Reduce heat and simmer, partially covered, for 15 minutes or until fennel is tender. Stir in chilled clam meat; reheat, but do not boil. Stir in salt, pepper and parsley. Taste and adjust seasonings as needed.

3. Pour cream into a large warmed soup tureen; whisk in egg yolk. Continue whisking and pour in about half of the hot broth; stir in remaining soup. Ladle into warmed soup bowls. Serve with a bowl of lemon wedges to pass at the table.

Roasted Tomato Bisque with Sea Salt Wedges

Serves 4

Roasting the tomatoes, onion and garlic in a very hot oven enhances and mingles all their flavors.

Tip

If the tomatoes are very ripe, here's a quick way to remove their seeds: turn tomato halves upside-down over a bowl and squeeze out the seeds. If they are not quite ripe enough, you will need to use your thumb or forefinger to pry the seeds away from the flesh.

- *Preheat oven to 450°F (230°C)*
- *Large baking sheet*

12 to 14	large plum tomatoes, cut in half lengthwise and seeded (for technique, see tip, at left)	12 to 14
1 tbsp	butter	15 mL
1	onion, diced	1
1	clove garlic, minced	1
2 cups	chicken stock	500 mL
1/8 tsp	cayenne pepper	0.5 mL
1/4 cup	chopped fresh basil	50 mL
1/4 tsp	salt	1 mL
8	Sea Salt Wedges (see recipe, page 32)	8

1. Arrange tomatoes cut-side up in a single layer on baking sheet. Roast on top rack in preheated oven for 20 minutes or until edges are browned; cool slightly. If skins stick to pan as tomatoes are removed, leave behind and discard.

2. In a large saucepan, heat butter over medium heat. Add onion and garlic; cook for 5 minutes or until softened. Add tomatoes, plus any juice from baking sheet, stock and cayenne; bring to a boil. Reduce heat and simmer, partially covered and stirring occasionally, for 15 minutes. In a blender or food processor, purée soup in batches; return to saucepan. Heat until hot; stir in half of the basil and salt. Taste and adjust seasonings as needed. Ladle into warmed soup bowls; garnish with a sprinkling of remaining basil. Serve with a basket of Sea Salt Wedges to pass at the table.

Garlicky Chunky Chicken Soup

This colorful, flavorful soup is perfect for serving to lunchtime guests. Just add salad and bread and your menu is set.

Tip

While it's possible to prepare this soup in advance, we think it's better made at the last minute so that the vegetables remain crunchy and the chicken does not get overcooked.

1 tbsp	olive oil or canola oil	15 mL
8 oz	skinless boneless chicken breasts or thighs	250 g
2	cloves garlic, minced	2
1	onion, diced	1
1	stalk celery, diced	1
1	carrot, diced	1
6 cups	chicken stock	1.5 L
1	bay leaf	1
1	sprig fresh thyme (or ¼ tsp/1 mL dried)	1
¼ tsp	black pepper	1 mL
1 cup	small broccoli florets or half bunch broccolini, cut into 1-inch (2.5 cm) pieces	250 mL
⅓ cup	grated Parmesan or Romano cheese	75 mL

1. In a large skillet, heat oil over medium-high heat. Add chicken and sauté for 5 minutes per side or until golden and just cooked. Remove chicken; reduce heat to medium. Add garlic and onion; cook for 5 minutes or until softened. Add celery and carrot; cook for 5 minutes. Transfer vegetable mixture to a large saucepan. Use some of the stock to deglaze the skillet; add to saucepan along with remaining stock, bay leaf and thyme; bring to a boil. Reduce heat and simmer, covered, for 15 minutes.

2. Meanwhile, cut chicken into cubes. When soup has finished simmering, add chicken, including any juices, along with pepper and broccoli. Simmer for 5 minutes or until hot and broccoli is just tender. Discard bay leaf and thyme sprig. Ladle into warmed soup bowls; serve garnished with a generous sprinkling of Parmesan.

Moroccan Cumin Chicken Soup

Terrifically tasty and rich in color and flavors, this spicy soup makes the perfect centerpiece for a lunchtime menu. Moroccans are passionate about their couscous, which they steam several times over boiling stock or water. We love couscous, too, for its ease of preparation and versatility — in soups, salads and main-course meals.

12 oz	skinless boneless chicken breasts or thighs	375 g
2 tsp	ground cumin	10 mL
1 to	olive oil or	15 to
2 tbsp	canola oil	25 mL
1	onion, diced	1
2	large carrots, diced	2
2	cloves garlic, minced	2
8 cups	chicken stock	2 L
½ tsp	salt	2 mL
¼ tsp	black pepper	1 mL
½ cup	dry uncooked couscous or 1 cup (250 mL) cold cooked rice	125 mL
1 tsp	lemon juice	5 mL
¼ cup	finely chopped fresh coriander or parsley	50 mL

1. Sprinkle both sides of chicken with ground cumin. In a large skillet, heat 1 tbsp (15 mL) oil over medium heat. Add chicken and sauté, using more oil if needed when turning, for 5 minutes per side or until golden. Transfer chicken to a plate. Add onion, carrots and garlic to the skillet; cook for 8 minutes or until softened. Transfer vegetable mixture to a large saucepan. Use some of the stock to deglaze skillet; add to saucepan along with remaining stock. Bring to a boil. Reduce heat and simmer, covered, for 15 minutes.

2. Meanwhile, cut chicken into cubes. When soup has finished simmering, add chicken, including any accumulated juices, along with salt, pepper, couscous and lemon juice. Simmer for 5 minutes; stir in coriander. Taste and adjust seasonings as needed. Ladle into warmed soup bowls.

Chili Lime Chicken Soup

It may seem curious that hot countries like Thailand should produce fiery-hot foods. But it makes sense when you consider that spicy foods induce sweating, which has the effect of lowering the body temperature. Here, the Thai influence of this almost fat-free soup can be found in the jolts of tiny fresh hot chilies, as well as a multitude of complex flavors accentuated with refreshing lime.

Tips

If you're not familiar with the powerful salty flavor of fish sauce, use it with caution! Start by adding it sparingly, then add more to taste.

Lime leaves are deep green, glossy and add an authentic flavor to this soup. They are sold in Oriental stores and some supermarkets. If you can't find any, grated lime zest makes a reasonably adequate replacement.

8 oz	skinless, boneless chicken breasts, very cold or partially frozen	250 g
2	stalks lemongrass, top third removed, white bulb lightly crushed	2
6 cups	unsalted chicken stock	1.5 L
4	lime leaves or grated zest of 1 lime	4
2	slices ginger root	2
2	cloves garlic, lightly crushed	2
1 or 2	tiny hot red chilies (Thai bird or finger peppers), seeded and very thinly sliced	1 or 2
1 cup	sliced button mushrooms	250 mL
	Juice of 1 lime	
1 tbsp	fish sauce	15 mL
¼ cup	coarsely chopped fresh coriander leaves	50 mL
2	green onions, thinly sliced	2

1. Slice chicken into thin strips. Keep refrigerated while preparing soup. In a large saucepan, stir together lemongrass, stock, lime leaves, ginger and garlic; bring to a boil over high heat. Reduce heat and simmer, covered, for 20 minutes. Remove lemongrass, lime leaves, ginger and garlic; discard. Increase heat to high; bring to a boil. Add chilies and mushrooms; drop in chicken strips one at a time (to avoid sticking). Reduce heat and simmer, uncovered, for 5 minutes or until chicken is cooked.

2. Stir in lime juice, fish sauce, coriander and green onions; ladle into warmed soup bowls. Serve traditional accompaniments — hot pepper sauce, lime wedges, and fish sauce — to add at the table.

Sole Velouté with Diced Vegetables

Whenever you see "velouté" in the title of a recipe, you can be sure it's an elegant, classic dish. Velouté means that the sauce or liquid is prepared from a roux of butter and flour, to which is slowly added a white stock made from fish, veal or chicken. This soup is dotted with myriad colors provided by a variety of vegetables. For maximum effect, be sure to dice them all the same size.

Tip

You can prepare this recipe in advance, to the end of Step 1. Cover and chill the velouté. When ready to serve, reheat to a simmer over low heat, stirring frequently. Add the mushroom and fish pieces and simmer for 5 minutes as directed.

2 tbsp	butter	25 mL
1	onion, diced	1
1	large carrot, diced	1
1	red bell pepper, seeded and diced	1
1	large stalk celery or fennel, diced	1
1/4 cup	all-purpose flour	50 mL
6 cups	fish stock or chicken stock, cooled	1.5 L
1/4 cup	dry white wine	50 mL
1	large slice ginger root	1
1	bay leaf	1
1/8 tsp	cayenne pepper	0.5 mL
4	large white mushrooms, thinly sliced	4
1 tsp	lemon juice	5 mL
1/4 tsp	salt	1 mL
1 lb	sole, cut into 1-inch (2.5 cm) chunks	500 g
1/4 cup	coarsely chopped fresh parsley	50 mL

1. In a large saucepan, melt butter over medium heat. Add onion, carrot, bell pepper and celery; cook, stirring occasionally, for 8 minutes or until softened. Sprinkle with flour. Slide pan off heat; slowly stir in stock and wine. Add ginger, bay leaf and cayenne; return to heat. Bring to a boil, stirring often. Reduce heat and simmer, covered, for 15 minutes. Remove ginger and bay leaf and discard.

2. Stir mushrooms, lemon juice and salt into soup. Taste and adjust seasonings as needed. Just before serving, stir in sole and half of the parsley; simmer, covered, for 5 minutes without stirring. Ladle into heated serving bowls; serve garnished with a sprinkling of remaining parsley.

When the temperature rises outdoors, there's nothing like a bowl of flavorful chilled soup to cool and refresh you! On days like these, you want to avoid anything hot — like a stove — so a number of our soups require no cooking. And most can be made ahead and kept in the refrigerator for a day or so. We've even included a breakfast soup — Banana Bisque (see page 158) — for those steamy days when appetites need an early morning lift.

Coolers

Pear and Parsnip Soup with Roasted Pepper 146

Minted Petits Pois Soup 147

Chilled Curried Carrot Soup 148

Fresh Tomato and Basil Soup with Olive Oil 149

Chilled Watercress Soup with Cucumber Raita 150

Yellow Pepper Soup with Fresh Tomato Salsa 152

No-Cook Avocado Soup 154

Fruit Soup with Fresh Basil 155

Breakfast Banana Bisque 156

Chilled Artichoke Soup 158

Balkan Beet and Buttermilk Soup 160

Cooling Cucumber Soup with Chives 161

Pear and Parsnip Soup with Roasted Pepper

Serves 4 to 6

Ever notice how pears seem to take ages to ripen and then, apparently overnight, become too soft? Well, here's a soup where you should use slightly overripe pears. Their intense flavor works beautifully with a much-overlooked vegetable — parsnips.

Tips

After peeling parsnips, drop them into a bowl of water acidified with lemon juice to prevent them from discoloring. But don't leave them in the water too long — they're extremely porous and will absorb too much water if left for more than a few minutes.

When cooked, parsnips have a silky texture and a sweet, smoky flavor. (Their high sugar content also makes parsnips ideal for roasting, since the sugar caramelizes quickly, intensifying their flavor.)

1 tbsp	butter	15 mL
2	ripe pears, peeled and sliced	2
Half	small onion, diced	Half
1	clove garlic, minced	1
1 lb	parsnips, peeled and sliced (see tip, at left)	500 g
1	roasted yellow, orange or red bell pepper, peeled and seeded	1
4 cups	chicken or vegetable stock	1 L
1/2 tsp	salt	2 mL
1/8 tsp	hot pepper sauce	0.5 mL
2 tbsp	finely chopped fresh parsley or basil	25 mL

1. In a large saucepan, melt butter over medium heat. Add pears, onion and garlic; cook for 5 minutes or until softened. Stir in parsnips, bell pepper and stock; bring to a boil. Reduce heat and simmer, covered, for 20 minutes or until parsnips are very tender.

2. In a blender or food processor, purée soup in batches; add salt and hot pepper sauce. Pour into a bowl and chill, covered, for 6 hours or overnight. Taste and adjust seasoning as needed. Ladle into chilled soup bowls; serve garnished with a sprinkling of parsley.

Minted Petits Pois Soup

Serves 6

Tiny petits pois are the darlings of French cuisine. Sadly, they are almost impossible to find in North America. So here, in an effort to duplicate their sweet flavor, we have substituted small green peas taken fresh from the pod. Peas that you shell yourself are best — in fact, you should always buy more than you need, since you're sure to eat a lot of them while you're shelling — but frozen ones are a fine second choice.

Tip

Classic French chefs often "steam" petits pois between two layers of lettuce leaves in a saucepan. The lettuce provides moisture necessary for steaming and is usually discarded after a few minutes of cooking. Here, we've used sturdy romaine lettuce and kept it as part of the purée.

1 tbsp	butter	15 mL
3	leeks, white and light green parts only, thinly sliced	3
2 cups	tiny fresh peas	500 mL
4 cups	hot chicken stock	1 L
½ tsp	salt	2 mL
1	medium head romaine lettuce, chopped	1
¼ cup	chopped fresh mint	50 mL
1 cup	whipping (35%) cream	250 mL
	Fresh mint sprigs	

1. In a large saucepan, melt butter over medium heat. Add leeks and cook for 5 minutes or until softened. Stir in peas, stock and salt. Reduce heat and simmer, uncovered, for 2 to 3 minutes or until peas are hot. Stir in lettuce and mint. When lettuce has just wilted, remove saucepan from heat.

2. In a blender or food processor, purée soup in batches. Transfer to a bowl and chill, covered, for 6 hours or overnight. When ready to serve, stir in cream. Taste and adjust seasoning as needed. Ladle into chilled soup bowls; serve garnished with mint sprigs.

Chilled Curried Carrot Soup

While you can use ground cumin for this soup, you'll get a much more intense flavor if you buy whole cumin seeds and toast them. Just heat a small dry cast-iron skillet over medium heat, toss in the cumin seeds and stir until they darken slightly. Cool, then store in an airtight container.

Tip

While this soup is wonderful on its own, try serving it with poppadums, the traditional thin, crisp Indian rounds that are available in Indian food stores and many supermarkets. There are many ways to toast them: held over a gas burner with tongs, moving it about as it puffs and crisps; microwaved on High for about 1 minute after brushing one side with a little olive oil; or, if you have no fear of fat, you can put about 3 inches (7.5 cm) of canola or peanut oil into a saucepan, heat over medium high; when hot, drop in one poppadum at a time for about 20 seconds.

2 tbsp	butter	25 mL
1	large Spanish onion or other sweet onion	1
1 tbsp	curry powder	15 mL
1 tsp	toasted cumin seeds (for technique, see note, at left) or ½ tsp (1 mL) ground cumin	5 mL
½ tsp	salt	2 mL
3 cups	chicken stock	750 mL
4 cups	sliced carrots	1 L
1	large baking potato, peeled and diced	1
1 to 2 cups	whole milk or half-and-half (10%) cream	250 to 500 mL
2 tbsp	chopped fresh coriander or parsley	25 mL
6 to 8	poppadums, toasted and crisp, optional (see tip, at left)	6 to 8

1. In a large saucepan, melt butter over medium heat. Add onion and cook for 5 minutes or until softened. Stir in curry powder, cumin and salt; cook for 2 to 3 minutes or until very fragrant. Stir in stock, carrots and potato; bring to a boil. Reduce heat and simmer, covered, for 15 to 20 minutes or until carrots are very tender.

2. In a food processor or blender, purée soup in batches. Transfer to a bowl and chill, covered, for 6 hours or overnight. When ready to serve, stir in half the milk. Taste and adjust seasonings as required; add more milk as needed to thin soup. Ladle into chilled soup bowls; garnish with a sprinkling of coriander. If desired, serve with a plate of poppadums to pass at the table.

Fresh Tomato and Basil Soup with Olive Oil

Serves 4

Late in the summer, when there are more tomatoes on the vine than we can possibly eat, we look for imaginative ways to use them up before the frost. This stellar soup nearly explodes with fresh tomato flavor.

Tip

Use your best quality extra virgin olive oil for drizzling on top. The difference in flavor is worth the extra pennies.

1 tbsp	olive oil	15 mL
2 tbsp	all-purpose flour	25 mL
1 tbsp	lemon juice	15 mL
½ cup	beef, vegetable or chicken stock	125 mL
6	large ripe tomatoes, cored, seeded and quartered, juice reserved	6
½ tsp	salt	2 mL
½ to 1 tsp	granulated sugar	2 to 5 mL
4 or 5	large fresh basil leaves	4 or 5
2 tbsp	extra virgin olive oil	25 mL
¼ cup	finely shredded fresh basil	50 mL

1. In a large saucepan, heat oil over medium heat. Sprinkle in flour and cook for 1 minute or until bubbly. Slide pan off heat. In a bowl stir together lemon juice and stock; whisk into flour mixture. When smooth, add tomatoes (with juice) and salt.

2. Return saucepan to heat and bring to a boil, stirring frequently; remove from heat. In a blender or food processor, purée soup in batches. Taste and stir in sugar and other seasonings as needed. Transfer to a bowl and chill, covered, for 6 hours or overnight. Ladle into chilled soup bowls; serve garnished with a drizzle of olive oil and a sprinkling of shredded basil.

Joan's Tip

I'm a real stickler about removing the skins of tomatoes before using them in cooking. (Marilyn, on the other hand, rarely removes the skins.) If you're like me, here's an easy way to remove skins: lower the tomatoes into boiling water, leave for 30 seconds, then transfer to a bowl of icy cold water. The skins will slip off easily. (This method works for peaches, too.)

Chilled Watercress Soup with Cucumber Raita

Tip

If you want to thicken the yogurt or sour cream for the raita, spoon it into a coffee-filter-lined cone or sieve and set over a bowl in the refrigerator for several hours. You'll be surprised at how much water drains off.

RAITA

Half	English cucumber, unpeeled	Half
1/2 cup	thick plain yogurt or sour cream	125 mL
1/4 tsp	salt	1 mL
Pinch	cayenne pepper	Pinch

SOUP

1 tbsp	butter	15 mL
1	small onion, diced	1
3 tbsp	all-purpose flour	45 mL
1/2 tsp	salt	2 mL
1/4 tsp	black pepper	1 mL
3 cups	chicken stock	750 mL
3	bunches watercress, coarse stems removed	3
1 cup	whipping (35%) cream or half-and-half (10%) cream	250 mL
	Watercress sprigs for garnish	

1. *Raita:* Grate unpeeled cucumber and, over a sink, squeeze out liquid with your hands. Transfer squeezed cucumber to a bowl. Stir in yogurt, salt and cayenne; cover and refrigerate.

2. *Soup:* In a large saucepan, melt butter over medium heat. Add onion and cook for 5 minutes or until onion has softened. Sprinkle in flour, salt and pepper; stir until absorbed. Slide pan off heat. Whisk stock into flour mixture; bring to a boil, stirring often. Add watercress leaves; simmer for 5 minutes.

3. In a blender or food processor, purée soup in batches. Transfer to a bowl and chill, covered, for 6 hours or overnight. Before serving, stir in cream. Taste and adjust seasoning as needed. Ladle into chilled soup bowls. Garnish with a dollop of Cucumber Raita in center, topped with a sprig of watercress.

Joan's Tip

When writing cookbooks, even the most successful author teams can have completely opposite opinions about how a dish should be finished. And here's a case in point: Marilyn simply purées the soup and chills it (as directed in Step 3). But I insert the extra step of forcing the puréed soup through a nylon sieve to trap any bits of watercress — which, as I still remember from a dinner party of long ago, have the embarrassing tendency to lodge between one's front teeth!

Yellow Pepper Soup with Fresh Tomato Salsa

Serves 4

All too often we see diced peppers garnishing tomato soup, so here's something of a role-reversal — a bell pepper soup complimented with a topping of spicy, crunchy tomato salsa. In keeping with the golden color of the saffron used to spice the soup, we decided to use yellow peppers here — but red or orange peppers can be used just as successfully.

- • *Preheat broiler or barbecue grill*

4	large yellow bell peppers	4
1 tbsp	butter	15 mL
1	onion, diced	1
1	large clove garlic, minced	1
2 cups	chicken stock	500 mL
1	large carrot, sliced	1
1	small banana pepper or jalapeño pepper, seeded	1
¼ tsp	saffron threads, crumbled	1 mL
1 cup	half-and-half (10%) cream	250 mL
½ cup	Fresh Salsa Topping (see recipe, page 33)	125 mL

1. Under broiler or on barbecue grill, roast peppers, turning occasionally, for 15 minutes or until skins are charred black. Place in a paper bag; close and leave in bag for 10 minutes. Peel and cut in half. Reserving juice, discard the stem, skin and seeds.

2. In a large saucepan, melt butter over medium heat. Add onion and garlic; cook for 5 minutes or until onion has softened. Stir in stock, carrot, roasted peppers (including juices) and banana pepper. Crumble in saffron; bring to a boil. Reduce heat and simmer, covered, for 20 minutes or until vegetables are very tender.

3. In a blender or food processor, purée soup in batches. Transfer to a bowl and chill, covered, for 6 hours or overnight. When ready to serve, stir in cream. Taste and adjust seasoning as needed. Ladle into chilled soup bowls; serve garnished with a spoonful of Fresh Salsa Topping.

No-Cook Avocado Soup

Serves 4

The only real challenge in this quick and easy soup is determining whether the avocado is ripe. It should be neither too hard nor too soft — yielding only slightly when squeezed — and its outer covering should be unblemished and turning dark. Most avocados sold in North America are of the excellent Hass (often misspelled as "Haas") variety, which turn black on the outside as they ripen but remain bright green and luscious inside.

Tip

While many recipes recommend adding lemon juice to prevent a peeled avocado from discoloring, it's not necessary here, since the acid in the yogurt or sour cream prevents it from darkening. Even so, the soup still should be served within 4 hours of preparation. Stir in the yogurt by hand after you have puréed the avocado and stock; using a blender or mixer will cause the yogurt to become liquid.

1	large avocado, peeled and pitted	1
1	small clove garlic, minced	1
1	green onion, sliced	1
1 tsp	lime juice	5 mL
1/4 cup	coriander or parsley leaves	50 mL
2 cups	cold chicken stock	500 mL
1/2 tsp	salt	2 mL
1/8 tsp	cayenne	0.5 mL
3/4 cup	thick yogurt or sour cream	175 mL
	Coriander leaves or toasted hazelnuts or avocado slices	

1. In a blender or food processor, purée avocado, garlic, onion, lime juice, coriander, stock, salt and cayenne. Transfer to a bowl; stir in yogurt. Refrigerate, covered, for 1 hour or until soup is chilled. Serve soup within 4 hours of preparation. Ladle into chilled soup bowls; garnish with a few whole coriander leaves, toasted hazelnuts or paper thin slices of avocado.

Fruit Soup with Fresh Basil

Serves 8

When fruit is plentiful and cheap, this no-cook fat-free soup makes the perfect light starter — or flavorful finale — to a summer meal on the patio or porch. Choose melons such as cantaloupe (or honeydew or watermelon), grapes, cherries, peaches, plums and nectarines. Berries such as strawberries, raspberries and blueberries add rich color. Aromatic fresh basil enhances the fruit flavors.

6 cups	raspberry, cranberry or apple juice	1.5 L
2 or 3	thin slices ginger root	2 or 3
1 tbsp	freshly squeezed lime or lemon juice	15 mL
6 to 8 cups	fresh bite-size fruit pieces (see note, at left, for suggestions)	1.5 to 2 L
¼ cup	finely shredded fresh basil	50 mL

1. In a large pitcher, combine raspberry juice, ginger and lime juice. Cover and refrigerate for several hours or overnight. When ready to serve, remove and discard ginger. Place fruit pieces and basil in a large clear bowl. Pour in juice mixture; gently stir. Ladle into chilled clear soup bowls.

Breakfast Banana Bisque

Serves 4

Fruit soups had a brief success as part of the nouvelle cuisine scene in the mid 1980s, but this one survives because it's such a good pick-me-up any time of the day. The cinnamon flavor marries beautifully with the banana.

Tips

Dieters can feel free to make this soup with skim milk; skinnies can use whole milk or cream — even whipping cream!

This soup makes an easy hot-weather breakfast for guests. Serve with baking powder biscuits, fruit preserves and deep-roasted coffee.

● *Preheat oven to 350°F (180°C)*

2 tbsp	butter	25 mL
2	slices bread, crusts removed and cut into ½-inch (1 cm) cubes	2
¼ tsp	cinnamon	1 mL
4	large bananas	4
1¼ cups	milk or cream	300 mL
½ tsp	cinnamon	2 mL

1. In a pie plate, melt butter in the preheated oven; add bread cubes and toss until coated. Bake, stirring twice, for 10 to 15 minutes or until golden. Sprinkle with ¼ tsp (1 mL) cinnamon; toss until coated.

2. In a blender or food processor, combine bananas, milk and ½ tsp (2 mL) cinnamon; blend until smooth. Pour into chilled bowls. Float a few warm croutons on top; serve immediately.

Chilled Artichoke Soup

Cooking with artichokes often requires a lot of work. But here's an artichoke soup that is sophisticated and creamy — and requires very little fuss. Since the soup needs time to chill before serving, it's a great make-ahead for when you're entertaining guests.

4	fresh artichokes	4
1	lemon, halved	1
1 tbsp	butter	15 mL
1	stalk celery, sliced	1
1	small onion, diced	1
1	baking potato, peeled and diced	1
4 cups	chicken stock	1 L
1	bay leaf	1
1	large sprig fresh thyme	1
1/4 tsp	crushed red pepper flakes	1 mL
1 cup	buttermilk or yogurt	250 mL
1 tsp	lemon juice	5 mL
1 tsp	salt	5 mL
1/4 tsp	black pepper	1 mL
1/2 cup	pumpernickel croutons (see recipe, page 30)	125 mL
2 tbsp	snipped chives or thinly sliced green onions	25 mL

1. Cut off stem and top third of pointed ends of artichoke. Cut in half lengthwise and, using a spoon, scrape out hairy choke. Immediately rub with lemon half to prevent browning. Set aside.

2. In a large saucepan, melt butter over medium heat. Add celery and onion; cook for 5 minutes or until softened. Add artichokes, potato, stock, bay leaf, thyme and pepper flakes; bring to a boil, stirring often. Reduce heat and simmer, covered, for 20 minutes.

3. In a blender or food processor, purée soup in batches. Force warm mixture through a fine mesh sieve into a bowl, discarding solids. Chill, covered, for 6 hours or overnight. Just before serving, stir in buttermilk, lemon juice, salt and pepper. Taste and adjust seasoning as needed. Ladle into chilled soup bowls; serve garnished with pumpernickel croutons and a sprinkling of snipped chives.

Balkan Beet and Buttermilk Soup

Serves 4

While English cucumbers are prized for their small-seeded interiors, I prefer the flavor of old-fashioned garden variety cukes. Peel them only if they've been waxed or skins taste bitter. Then split them lengthwise and scoop out and discard the seedy interior before dicing.

Tip

Commercially produced buttermilk is made from 1% or 2% milk and gets its silky creaminess from having been cultured with friendly bacteria in the same manner as yogurt or sour cream.

¼ cup	light sour cream	50 mL
¼ cup	low-fat cottage cheese	50 mL
2 cups	buttermilk	500 mL
¼ cup	chopped fresh parsley	50 mL
¼ tsp	salt	1 mL
¼ tsp	black pepper	1 mL
2	cooked beets, diced	2
1 cup	diced cucumber (see note, at left)	250 mL
2	large radishes, thinly sliced	2
1	green onion, thinly sliced	1
	Hot pepper sauce	

1. In a blender or food processor, combine sour cream, cottage cheese and buttermilk; purée until smooth. Add parsley, salt and pepper; pulse on and off a few times just until mixed. Taste and adjust seasonings as needed. Divide beets, cucumber and radishes among chilled bowls. Pour soup over vegetables; garnish with a sprinkling of green onion. Serve with a bottle of hot pepper sauce to pass at the table.

Marilyn's Note

When I cooked and baked at a spa in the early 1990s, just as the low-fat-food fad began, my wildly creative colleagues and I developed our own low-fat recipes because there were few published ones to draw upon. This is one of our creations.

Yellow Pepper Soup with Fresh Tomato Salsa • *page 152*

Cooling Cucumber Soup with Chives

Serves 6

When the thermometer soars and nobody wants to turn on the stove, here's a cooling soup that requires no cooking.

Tip

Buttermilk is very creamy and, despite its name, has no more fat than 1% or 2% milk. If, instead of buttermilk, you are using yogurt thinned with milk, add milk gradually to the yogurt, whisking constantly.

2	cucumbers	2
4 cups	cultured buttermilk or 2 cups (500 mL) each of thick plain yogurt and milk	1 L
½ tsp	finely grated lime or lemon zest	2 mL
½ tsp	salt	2 mL
¼ tsp	hot pepper sauce	1 mL
2 tbsp	snipped chives or thinly sliced green onions	25 mL

1. If cucumbers are waxed, peel them; otherwise leave skins on. Slice off and discard ends. Cut cucumbers in half lengthwise. With a spoon, scoop out and discard soft seeded area. Finely grate cucumber or chop coarsely in a food processor. Transfer to a fine sieve and allow liquid to drain for 15 minutes.

2. Transfer drained cucumber to a large bowl; stir in buttermilk. Add zest, salt and hot pepper sauce; refrigerate, covered, for 2 hours or until chilled. Ladle into chilled soup bowls; serve garnished with a sprinkling of chives.

Vietnamese Pho Soup • *page 176*

In a perfect world, all soups would be made from only the best stock, with only the freshest ingredients. But all too often we just don't have the time. Here we provide recipes that use canned soups, crab, tomatoes and other ingredients to create ultra-fast soups that are delicious enough to serve to guests. One warning: canned soups tend to be quite salty, so wait until just before serving to taste if any more salt is needed.

Jump Starts

Tomato Soup with Tortellini 164

Clear Tortellini and Spinach Soup 165

Clam Chowder with Roasted Garlic 166

Broccoli and Cheddar Chowder. 167

French Canadian Pea Soup
    with Bacon and Fresh Thyme 168

Chunky Cream of Vegetable Soup 169

Charleston Crab Soup. 170

Granny Smith Squash Soup. 171

Cajun Tomato Soup. 172

Tex-Mex Chili Soup. 173

Mediterranean Mussel and Tomato Soup 174

Vietnamese Pho Soup 176

Portobello Mushroom Soup with Sherry 177

New Orleans Gumbo 178

Avocado Soup with Lime. 179

Pea Soup Diable. 180

Curried Chicken Soup with Toasted Coconut 181

Cucumber Yogurt Soup 182

Mushroom Consommé 183

Tomato Soup with Tortellini

Serves 16

Served in mugs with a stir stick for spearing the tortellini treat at the bottom of the cup, this soup is perfect for warming up a crowd at a skating party or after a day on the ski slopes or trails.

4 cups	chicken stock	1 L
1	can (48 oz/1.36 L) tomato or vegetable juice	1
1	can (28 oz/796 mL) diced tomatoes, with juice	1
2	zucchini, diced	2
1	green bell pepper, seeded and diced	1
8	stalks celery, diced	8
1	large onion, diced	1
¼ cup	chopped fresh basil	50 mL
¼ tsp	black pepper	1 mL
2 cups	fresh or frozen cheese tortellini	500 mL
½ cup	chopped fresh parsley	125 mL

1. In a large pot, combine stock, juice, tomatoes (with juice), zucchini, green pepper, celery, onion and basil. Bring to a boil over medium heat, stirring occasionally. Reduce heat and simmer, partly covered and stirring occasionally, for 30 minutes.

2. In a blender or food processor, purée soup in batches; return to pot. Add black pepper; heat until hot. Taste and adjust seasonings as needed. Stir in tortellini; simmer for 15 minutes or until cooked. Stir in half of the parsley. Ladle into warmed soup bowls; serve garnished with a sprinkling of remaining parsley.

Joan's Note

My sister, Carol McGonigal, adapted this recipe from a cookbook published by the Kinsmen Reh-Fit Centre in Winnipeg. Every Friday, Carol and a few of her teacher colleagues went to the same restaurant for lunch, where she enjoyed a tomato soup with tortellini similar to this recipe.

Clear Tortellini and Spinach Soup

With a bag of frozen tortellini in the freezer, you've got more than a meal-in-a-minute waiting for you! Just combine it with clear broth and spinach and you'll have an up-market soup that's fit for company.

1	can (10 oz/284 mL) chicken broth, plus one can of water	1
1 cup	fresh or frozen cheese or meat tortellini	250 mL
1 cup	shredded fresh spinach	250 mL
2 tbsp	dry white wine	25 mL
2 tbsp	grated Parmesan cheese	25 mL

1. In a medium saucepan, combine canned broth and water. Bring to a boil over high heat. Stir in tortellini and simmer, partially covered, for 10 to 12 minutes or until tender. Stir in spinach and white wine; heat until hot. Ladle into warmed soup bowls; serve garnished with a sprinkling of Parmesan cheese.

Clam Chowder
with Roasted Garlic

Nobody will know you've "cheated" when you serve up this fragrant and flavorful chowder. Canned clams are almost as good as fresh. Just be sure to discard the clam juice; it's too salty to add to canned soup.

1	can (10 oz/284 mL) cream of potato with roasted garlic soup, plus one can of water	1
Half	red bell pepper, seeded and finely diced	Half
1	can (5 oz/142 g) baby clams, drained	1
¼ tsp	finely chopped fresh dill (or ⅛ tsp/0.5 mL dried)	1 mL

1. In a medium saucepan, combine canned soup, water and bell pepper. Bring to a boil over high heat. Stir in clams; heat until hot. Stir in dill. Ladle into warm bowls; serve garnished with a grinding of black pepper.

Broccoli and Cheddar Chowder

Serves 4

As kids we all knew that cheese sauce made broccoli edible! That comforting combination is revisited in this colorful textured soup, brimming with tiny broccoli florets.

1	can (10 oz/284 mL) cream of potato with roasted garlic soup, plus one can of milk	1
1	can (10 oz/284 mL) Cheddar soup, plus one can of water	1
2 cups	broccoli florets, cut very small	500 mL
1/8 tsp	cayenne pepper	0.5 mL
1/2 cup	pumpernickel croutons (see recipe, page 30)	125 mL

1. In a saucepan combine potato soup and milk with Cheddar soup and water. Bring just to a boil; stir in broccoli and cayenne. Heat until hot. Ladle into warmed soup bowls; serve garnished with pumpernickel croutons.

French Canadian Pea Soup with Bacon and Fresh Thyme

Whenever we have leftover bacon, we freeze it so that we always have some on hand to crumble on top of soups and salads. Its smoky flavor and crunchy texture help to pump up this canned soup, while adding extra herbs personalizes it. Be sure to use real bacon; prepackaged "bacon bits" are a poor imitation.

1	can (10 oz/284 mL) French Canadian pea or green pea soup, plus one can of water	1
1	carrot, finely grated	1
¼ tsp	chopped fresh thyme or pinch dried leaf thyme	1 mL
2	slices bacon, cooked crisp and crumbled	2

1. In a saucepan, combine canned soup and water with carrot and thyme. Bring to a boil. Ladle into warmed soup bowls; serve garnished with crumbled bacon.

Chunky Cream of Vegetable Soup

You'll want to serve this hearty, creamy soup on a chilly day. It's great to look at, terrifically tasty and it's also jam-packed with nutritious ingredients, making it an all-round winner.

1	can (10 oz/284 mL) cream of asparagus or mushroom soup, plus one can of whole milk	1
3 cups	frozen stir-fry or mixed vegetables	750 mL
1 tsp	lemon juice	5 mL
2 tbsp	chopped fresh parsley	25 mL

1. In a medium saucepan, combine canned soup and milk. Bring to a boil over medium–high heat; stir in frozen vegetables. Reduce heat and simmer for 5 minutes. Stir in lemon juice. Ladle into warmed soup bowls; serve garnished with a sprinkling of parsley.

Charleston Crab Soup

This easy-but-sophisticated soup combines many flavors from the American Deep South. Canned crab provides richness and texture. It's a versatile staple to have on hand for use in other soups, as well as salads and hors d'oeuvres; your friends will think you're such an imaginative and talented cook!

2	cans (each 10 oz/284 mL) cream of wild mushroom soup	2
1	soup can (10 oz/284 mL) half-and-half (10%) cream	1
1½ cups	water	375 mL
½ cup	finely chopped red bell pepper	125 mL
½ tsp	Worcestershire sauce	2 mL
⅛ tsp	hot pepper sauce	0.5 mL
1	can (about 4 oz/120g) crabmeat, well-drained	1
1 tsp	dry sherry	5 mL
1	green onion, thinly sliced	1
1 tbsp	finely chopped parsley	15 mL

1. In a saucepan combine canned soup, cream and water. Stir in bell pepper, Worcestershire sauce and hot pepper sauce. Bring to a boil; stir in crabmeat, sherry and green onion. Ladle into warmed soup bowls; serve garnished with a sprinkling of parsley.

Granny Smith Squash Soup

Serves 4

There are many foods that naturally complement each other; one such pairing is apples and squash. A package of frozen squash takes up very little room in the freezer but can turn an ordinary soup into something special.

1 tbsp	butter	15 mL
¼ cup	finely chopped onion	50 mL
1	pkg (14 oz/400 g) frozen puréed squash or 2 cups (500 mL) cooked thick puréed squash	1
1	can (10 oz/284 mL) chicken broth, plus one can of water	1
1	unpeeled green Granny Smith apple, grated	1
2 tbsp	finely chopped fresh coriander or ⅛ tsp (0.5 mL) grated nutmeg	25 mL

1. In a saucepan melt butter over medium heat. Add onion and cook for 3 minutes or until softened. Stir in squash, broth (and water) and apple; bring to a boil. Reduce heat and simmer for 5 minutes. Ladle into warmed soup bowls; serve garnished with a sprinkling of fresh coriander or grating of nutmeg

Cajun Tomato Soup

With a few simple additions, you can put your own special stamp on humble tomato soup, transforming it into an elevated experience. Such culinary make-overs need not be restricted to canned soup. Canned tomatoes are also a great starting point for creativity, too. Herbs that pair well with tomatoes include thyme, oregano, basil and marjoram.

1 tbsp	butter	15 mL
¼ cup	diced onion	50 mL
Half	jalapeño or banana pepper, seeded and finely diced or ¼ tsp (1 mL) hot pepper sauce	Half
1	can (10 oz/284 mL) tomato soup, plus one can of water	1
1 tsp	lime juice	5 mL
1	tomato, seeded and finely diced	1
2 tbsp	sour cream	25 mL
1 tbsp	finely chopped fresh coriander	15 mL

1. In a saucepan melt butter over medium heat. Add onion and hot pepper; cook for 3 minutes or until softened. Stir in canned soup and water; bring to a boil. Stir in lime juice and tomato. Ladle into warmed soup bowls; serve garnished with a dollop of sour cream and a sprinkling of fresh coriander.

Tex-Mex Chili Soup

Serves 3 to 4

If you love chili con carne, you'll be sure to want a second bowl of this piquant, chili-laced soup. Add a salad, some warm flour tortillas and you've got a complete meal.

1 tbsp	canola oil	15 mL
1	onion, diced	1
1	clove garlic, minced	1
1 tsp	chili powder	5 mL
1	can (10 oz/284 mL) tomato soup, plus one can of water	1
1 cup	hot salsa	250 mL
1	can (15.5 oz/439 g or 19 oz/540 mL) pinto, romano or red kidney beans, drained	1
¼ cup	sour cream	50 mL
2 tbsp	fresh chopped coriander	25 mL
	Tortilla chips	
	Hot pepper sauce	

1. In a large saucepan, heat oil over medium heat. Add onion and garlic; cook for 5 minutes or until softened. Stir in chili powder; cook for 1 minute. Add canned soup, water, salsa and drained beans; cover and simmer for 5 minutes. Ladle into warmed soup bowls; serve garnished with a dollop of sour cream and a sprinkling of coriander. Serve with tortilla chips and a bottle of hot pepper sauce to pass at the table.

Mediterranean Mussel and Tomato Soup

Serves 3 to 4

Add bread and salad and you've got a meal in minutes. It comes to us from Kaija Lind of Ship Harbour, Nova Scotia. As co-owner (with John Stairs) of Aquaprime Mussel Ranch, Kaija knows her mussels. They ship their sweet cold-water mussels to New York, San Francisco, Scotland, Iceland and all over Canada. Farmed mussels are grown off the bottom of the sea bed, so they're free of grit and ready-to-use. They're also healthy — low in fat, high in protein and contain Omega-3 fatty acids.

1 tbsp	olive oil	15 mL
1	onion, diced	1
2	cloves garlic, minced	2
1	can (28 oz/796 mL) diced tomatoes, including juice	1
½ cup	dry red or white wine	125 mL
½ tsp	dried leaf thyme	2 mL
½ tsp	dried basil	2 mL
1	bag (2 to 3 lbs/1 to 1.5 kg) fresh mussels	1
½ tsp	lemon juice	2 mL

1. In a large saucepan, heat oil over medium heat. Add onion and garlic; cook for 5 minutes or until softened. Stir in tomatoes, wine, thyme and basil. Increase heat to medium–high and bring to a boil. Add mussels; cover tightly and cook for 6 to 8 minutes or until shells open. Stir in lemon juice. Discard any mussels that do not open. Ladle, shells and all, into warmed shallow soup bowls. Serve with a pepper grinder to pass at the table.

Vietnamese Pho Soup

Serves 4

Pho soup is so easy to make! The meat is cooked just by the hot broth, ensuring that even very lean beef is very tender and flavorful. The fish sauce contains a lot of salt, so it's best to use reduced-salt beef broth, such as Campbell's Healthy Request, or consommé.

4 oz	lean boneless top round or sirloin steak	125 g
4 oz	thin rice stick noodles	125 g
2	cans (each 10 oz/284 mL) reduced-salt beef broth or consommé, plus two cans of water	2
1	2-inch (5 cm) piece ginger root, sliced	1
1 tbsp	fish sauce	15 mL
2	large mushrooms, thinly sliced	2
2	green onions, thinly sliced	2
1 cup	bean sprouts or julienned snow peas	250 mL
1 tsp	lime juice	5 mL

1. Place uncovered meat on a piece of foil; chill in freezer for 15 minutes or until firm but not frozen. Meanwhile, generously cover noodles with hot water and allow to soak for 15 minutes.

2. While noodles are soaking, combine broth and water with ginger and fish sauce in a large pot; bring to a boil. Reduce heat and simmer, covered, for 5 to 10 minutes. Meanwhile, very thinly slice partially-frozen meat; place raw slices in bottoms of warmed deep soup bowls. Drain noodles; divide among bowls. Scatter mushrooms, green onions and bean sprouts in bowls. Remove ginger from broth and discard; stir in lime juice. Bring broth to a rolling boil; ladle into bowls. (The heat from the boiling broth will cook the meat.) Serve with bottles of lime juice, fish sauce and hot pepper sauce to pass at the table.

Portobello Mushroom Soup with Sherry

Serves 3 to 4

With its intense flavors, this is a soup that you can serve with confidence to guests when you want to make a really good impression. The recipe is easily doubled for large dinner parties.

1 tbsp	butter	15 mL
1	onion, diced	1
1	stalk celery, diced	1
1	can (10 oz/284 mL) chicken broth, plus one can of water	1
2 tbsp	dry sherry	25 mL
1	large portobello mushroom, sliced	1
8	large button mushrooms, thinly sliced	8
½ cup	whipping (35%) cream	125 mL
2	green onions, thinly sliced	2

1. In a saucepan melt butter over medium heat. Add onion and celery; cook for 5 minutes or until softened. Stir in canned broth and water and sherry; add portobello mushroom slices. Bring to a boil; cover and simmer for 5 minutes. In a blender or food processor purée soup in batches; return to saucepan. Stir in button mushroom slices and cream; heat until hot, stirring frequently. Ladle into warmed soup bowls; serve garnished with a sprinkling of green onions. Serve with a pepper grinder to pass at the table.

New Orleans Gumbo

Load your CD player with some dixieland jazz, light the candles and savor the taste of old New Orleans. This soup also makes a great luncheon dish; serve it with some hot baking-powder biscuits and butter, then watch your family and friends ask for more.

1	can (10 oz/284 mL) chicken gumbo soup, plus one can of water	1
1 tsp	lemon juice	5 mL
4 oz	salad shrimp	125 g
1	tomato, seeded and diced	1
2	green onions, thinly sliced	2
2 tbsp	chopped fresh parsley	25 mL

1. In a medium saucepan, bring canned soup and water to a boil. Stir in lemon juice, shrimp, tomato and green onions; heat until hot. Ladle into warmed soup bowls; serve garnished with a sprinkling of parsley.

Avocado Soup with Lime

We love avocado and wondered if we could grate it into a soup and have it hold its color and shape. You can imagine our delight when we came up with this colorful and delicious winner. We're also nuts about lime juice and, in our own kitchen, would add more. We suggest starting with a small amount, adding more to suit your taste.

1	can (10 oz/284 mL) cream of chicken soup, plus one can of water	1
1	ripe avocado, peeled and grated	1
1/2 to 1 tsp	lime juice	2 to 5 mL
1/4 tsp	nutmeg	1 mL
1	green onion, thinly sliced	1

1. In a medium saucepan over medium heat, bring canned soup and water to a boil. Stir in avocado, 1/2 tsp (2 mL) lime juice and nutmeg; heat until hot. Taste and, if desired, add some or all of the remaining lime juice. Ladle into warmed soup bowls; serve garnished with a sprinkling of green onions.

Pea Soup Diable

Serves 3 to 4

1	can (10 oz/284 mL) green pea or French Canadian pea soup, plus one can of water	1
1	small carrot, finely grated	1
½ tsp	Dijon mustard	2 mL
¼ tsp	hot pepper sauce	1 mL
1 cup	diced ham or shredded deli-sliced ham	250 mL
½ tsp	lemon juice	2 mL
1 tbsp	chopped fresh parsley	15 mL

1. In a medium saucepan, combine canned soup and water with carrot, mustard and hot pepper sauce. Bring to a boil over medium heat. Stir in diced ham and lemon juice; heat until hot. Ladle into warmed soup bowls; serve garnished with a sprinkling of parsley.

Joan's Note

I remember loving a soup like this when I was a child. As an adult, I still love the flavor — and how easy it is to prepare! Canned soup combined with Dijon mustard (making it hot like the diable or devil) and deli-sliced ham will fool most people into thinking you made this soup from scratch. You won't need to add any salt to this soup; in fact, I like it better with "reduced salt" ham.

Curried Chicken Soup with Toasted Coconut

Supplementing cream of chicken soup with diced cooked chicken packs a nutritious protein wallop into every bowl. A touch of curry and a sprinkling of toasted coconut delivers Indian pizzazz.

Tip

If possible, use short, unsweetened coconut. To toast, spread out coconut on a baking pan; bake in a preheated 350°F (180°C) oven for about 5 minutes, stirring frequently, or until golden in color. Toasted coconut will keep for months in an airtight container.

1	can (10 oz/284 mL) cream of chicken soup, plus one can of milk	1
1 tsp	curry powder	5 mL
1 cup	diced cooked chicken or slivered deli-sliced chicken	250 mL
1	green onion, thinly sliced	1
1/2 tsp	lemon juice	2 mL
1/4 cup	toasted unsweetened coconut	50 mL
	Hot pepper sauce	

1. In a medium saucepan, combine canned soup and milk with curry powder. Bring to a boil over medium heat. Stir in chicken, green onion and lemon juice; heat until hot. Ladle into warmed soup bowls; garnish with a sprinkling of toasted coconut. Serve with a bottle of hot pepper sauce to pass at the table.

Cucumber Yogurt Soup

On a hot summer's day, a cooling bowl of this soup is guaranteed to refresh you. Peel the cucumber only if it has been waxed or the skin tastes bitter — but do get rid of all the seeds.

Tip

Remember never to process yogurt in a blender or food processor or it will thin out. Stir it into the soup after you've finished blending the ingredients.

1	can (10 oz/284 mL) chicken with rice soup	1
1	English cucumber (or regular cucumber, seeds removed), cut into large cubes	1
⅛ tsp	cayenne pepper	0.5 mL
½ cup	yogurt	125 mL
1 tbsp	chopped fresh parsley	15 mL

1. In a blender or food processor, combine soup, cucumber cubes and cayenne; purée until smooth. Transfer to a bowl and chill, covered, for 2 hours or until cold. Stir in yogurt. Ladle into chilled soup bowls; serve garnished with a sprinkling of parsley.

Mushroom Consommé

Serves 4

Consommé has always been regarded as a soup of some elegance. Here, we've developed a fit-for-entertaining soup using reduced-salt beef broth (we've had success with the Campbell's Healthy Request brand), which we find more flavorful than many beef stocks. The mushrooms and green onions are taste — and appearance — enhancers. This guilt-free soup is reminiscent of the best spa-food offerings and it is the perfect starter for a rich meal.

2	cans (each 10 oz/284 mL) reduced-salt beef broth or consommé, plus 2 cans of water	2
2 tsp	lemon juice	10 mL
4 oz	mushrooms, sliced	125 g
4	green onions, thinly sliced	4

1. In a medium saucepan, bring canned soup and water to a boil. Stir in lemon juice, mushrooms and green onions; heat until hot. Ladle into warmed soup bowls.

Library and Archives Canada Cataloguing in Publication

Crowley, Marilyn
    125 best soup recipes / Marilyn Crowley & Joan Mackie.

Previously published under title: The best soup cookbook.
ISBN 0-7788-0128-4

1. Soups.
I. Mackie, Joan II. Crowley, Marilyn. Best soup cookbook. III. Title.
IV. Title: One hundred twenty-five best soup recipes.

TX757.C76 2005   641.8'13   C2005-902577-8

Index

A

Acorn squash, with toasted seeds soup, 111
Apple cider, and curried squash soup, 110
Arame, miso soup, 85
Artichoke soup, 158
Asparagus
about, 68
and leek soup with new potatoes, 67
and pea soup, 69
soup, 68
Autumn leek soup, 64
Avocado soup, 154
with lime, 179

B

Bacon
French Canadian pea soup with, 168
scallop chowder with, 90
Balkan beet and buttermilk soup, 160
Banana bisque, 156
Barley
with lamb sausage chowder, 88
Scotch broth, 60
white bean soup with, 123
Bean and pasta soup, 54
Beef, stock, 22
Beefsteak, Vietnamese pho soup, 176
Beet and buttermilk soup, 160
Bell peppers
with fresh tomato salsa, 152
and white bean soup with barley, 123
Bisque
banana, 156
lobster, 56
roasted red pepper, 75
roasted tomato, 138
shrimp, 56
Black beans
preparation of, 124
soup, 124

Bouillabaisse, with fennel and rouille, 58
Bouquet garni, 17
Brazilian black bean soup, 124
Bread
croutons, 30
garlic, 28, 29
Breakfast banana bisque, 156
Broccoli
and Cheddar chowder, 103, 167
chicken soup, 139
Buttermilk
about, 160
cucumber soup, 161
Butternut squash, with toasted seeds soup, 111
Butters
flavored coins, 41
garlic, 28

C

Cabbage, sausage soup, 81
Cajun shrimp gazpacho, 51
Cajun tomato soup, 172
Cambozola, fennel soup with, 116
Carrots
curried soup, 148
Finnish vegetable soup, 66
soup with peanut sauce, 115
Cauliflower
Finnish vegetable soup, 66
and potato soup curried, 77
soup with Stilton, 78
Celeriac
and celery soup, 118
potato soup with julienne, 114
Celery, and celeriac soup, 118
Celestine crêpes, 37
chicken soup with, 128
Charleston crab soup, 170
Charmoula, 38
Cheddar cheese
and broccoli chowder, 103, 167
and corn chowder, 104

Cheese. See also specific cheeses
and basil snacks, 36
and garlic snacks, 36
Chicken. See also Chicken breasts; Chicken thighs
cooked, stock, 18
fresh bones stock, 20
gumbo soup, New Orleans–style, 178
soup, curried, 181
whole, stock, 16
Chicken breasts
and broccoli soup, 139
chili lime soup, 141
Moroccan cumin soup, 140
noodle soup, 48, 53
soup with Celestine crêpes, 128
Chicken thighs
Moroccan cumin soup, 140
noodle soup, 53
soup with broccoli, 139
Chickpeas
and spinach in broth, 82
and spinach soup, 80
Chili lime chicken soup, 141
Chilled artichoke soup, 158
Chilled curried carrot soup, 148
Chorizo, savoy soup, 81
Chowder
barley with lamb sausage, 88
broccoli and Cheddar cheese, 103, 167
clam, 96, 97, 166
corn and Cheddar cheese, 104
corn and kielbasa, 92
mushroom with Swiss cheese, 93
mussel with potatoes, 89
scallop with bacon, 90
seafood, 102
tomato clam, 97
two-salmon, 98
Chunky chicken noodle soup, 53
Chunky cream of vegetable soup, 169

Clams
    bouillabaisse, 58
    chowder, 96
    chowder with roasted garlic,
        166
    tomato chowder, 97
    and vegetable soup, 136
Clear corn soup, 84
Coconut milk
    about, 112
    roasted red pepper soup with,
        71
    Thai chowder with shrimp,
        100
Cold soups, 146–61
    artichoke, 158
    avocado, 154
    banana bisque, 156
    beet and buttermilk, 160
    chili lime chicken, 141
    cucumber, 161
    curried carrot, 148
    fruit with basil, 155
    pear and parsnip, 146
    petits pois, 147
    tomato and basil, 149
    watercress with cucumber
        raita, 150
    yellow pepper with tomato
        salsa, 152
Coriander, charmoula, 38
Corn
    and Cheddar cheese chowder,
        104
    chili bean soup with, 122
    and kielbasa chowder, 92
    soup, 84
Court bouillon, 24
Crab soup, 170
Cream soups
    carrot with peanut sauce,
        115
    cauliflower with Stilton, 78
    celery and celeriac soup,
        118
    corn 'n' Cheddar chowder,
        104
    Jerusalem artichoke with
        rouille, 119
    spinach with nutmeg and
        yogurt, 79
    vegetable, 169

    watercress with sea scallops,
        129
Crème fraîche, 40
Cremini mushroom soup, 117
Crêpes, celestine, 37
Crisps, parsnip, 34
Croutons, 30
Crunchy wedges, 32
Cucumber
    about, 160
    raita, 150
    soup with chives, 161
    yogurt soup, 182
Curry(ied)
    butter coins, 41
    carrot soup, 148
    cauliflower and potato soup,
        77
    chicken soup with coconut,
        181
    croutons, 30
    squash and cider soup, 110

D

Dijon vichyssoise, 46
Dill
    butter coins, 41
    and parsley pick-ups, 38
    two-salmon chowder, 98
Down-East clam chowder, 96

E

Egg noodles, chicken soup, 48,
    53
Eggs, celestine crêpes, 37

F

Fennel, soup with Cambozola,
    116
Fiery pumpkin soup with
    shrimp, 112
Finnish vegetable soup, 66
Fish
    court bouillon, 24
    stock, 25
Fish fillets
    bouillabaisse, 58
    seafood chowder, 102
Fish sauce, about, 112

Flavored butter coins, 41
Focaccia, 43
French bread croutons, 30
French Canadian pea soup
    with bacon, 168
    with ham, 61
French sweet onion soup, 50
Fresh clam and fall vegetable
    soup, 136
Fresh tomato and basil soup,
    149
Fresh tomato salsa, 33
Fresh tomato soup with
    cayenne mayonnaise, 65
Fruit soup with basil, 155

G

Garlic
    boats, 29
    bread, 28, 29
    butter, 28
    chunky chicken soup, 143
    croutons, 30
    spinach and beans in broth,
        82
    toasts, 29
Gazpacho, Cajun shrimp, 51
Ginger chicken noodle soup,
    48
Gorgonzola, fennel soup with,
    116
Granny Smith squash soup, 171
Gremolata, 38
Gumbo, New Orleans, 178

H

Ham, French Canadian pea
    soup with, 61
Ham bone stock, 21
Hazelnuts
    cremini mushroom soup, 117
    toasting, 117
Herb croutons, 30
Herbed crunchy wedges, 32
Horseradish butter coins, 41
Hot peppers
    about, 112
    rouille, 39
Hubbard squash, with toasted
    seeds soup, 111

I

Italian sausage
  barley chowder, 88
  lentil soup with, 121
  savoy soup, 81
Italian-style, croutons, 30

J

Jerusalem artichokes, soup with
    rouille, 119
Julentini soup, 108

K

Kidney beans
  chili and corn soup, 122
  and pasta soup, 54
  Tex-Mex soup, 173
Knockwurst, and corn chowder,
    92
Kombu, miso soup, 85

L

Lamb
  sausage, barley chowder, 88
  Scotch broth, 60
Landlocked bouillabaisse, 58
Leek(s)
  about, 46
  asparagus and new potato
    soup, 67
  butternut squash soup, 111
  celeriac potato soup, 114
  Dijon vichyssoise, 46
  petits pois soup, 147
  seeing double soup, 132
  soup, 64
Lentil
  dal soup, 120
  soup, 108
  soup with sausage, 121
Lime, butter coins, 41
Linguiça, savoy soup, 81
Lobster
  bisque, 56
  bouillabaisse, 58

M

Macaroni and bean soup, 54

Mayo and chives snacks, 36
Mediterranean mussel and
    tomato soup, 174
Mexican chili bean and corn
    soup, 122
Middle Eastern–style snacks, 36
Minestrone, 52
Minted petits pois soup, 147
Miso soup, 85
Moroccan-style
  croutons, 30
  cumin chicken soup, 140
Mozzarella cheese, lentil soup,
    108
Mushroom
  chowder with Swiss cheese,
    93
  consommé, 183
  leek soup, 64
  soup, 117
  soup with puff pastry dome,
    130
  soup with sherry, 177
Mussels
  bouillabaisse, 58
  chowder, 89, 97
  tomato chowder, 97
  and tomato soup, 174
  and vegetable soup, 136

N

New Orleans gumbo, 178
No-cook avocado soup, 154
Noodles, chicken soup, 48, 53

O

Onions. *See also* Sweet onions
  French sweet onion soup, 50
  and roasted carrot soup, 76
Orange, sweet potato soup with
    crème fraîche, 134
Oven-roasted vegetable soup,
    70

P

Parmesan
  croutons, 30
  curls, 72
  shortbreads, 42

Parsley
  butter coins, 41
  pick-ups, 38
Parsnip(s)
  crisps, 34
  and pear soup, 146
  vichyssoise with prosciutto,
    47
Pasta e fagioli, 54
Pear and parsnip soup with
    roasted pepper, 146
Pea(s)
  and asparagus soup, 69
  soup, 147
  soup diable, 180
Pesto, butter coins, 41
Pinto beans, Tex-Mex soup, 173
Pita breads, crunchy wedges, 32
Portobello mushroom soup
    with sherry, 177
Potato(es)
  about, 46
  asparagus and leek soup, 67
  and celeriac soup, 114
  clam chowder, 96
  corn and Cheddar cheese
    chowder, 104
  corn and kielbasa chowder,
    92
  and curried cauliflower soup,
    77
  Dijon vichyssoise, 46
  mussel chowder with, 89
  salmon chowder, 98
  scallop chowder with bacon,
    90
  spinach soup with yogurt, 79
Prosciutto
  parsnip vichyssoise, 47
  and pea soup, 125
Puff pastry, mushroom soup
    with, 130
Pumpernickel croutons, 30
Pumpkin soup with shrimp, 112

R

Raita, cucumber, 150
Rice
  about, 115
  carrot soup with peanut sauce
    and, 115

Rice noodles
   chowder with shrimp and coconut milk, 100
   Vietnamese pho soup, 176
Roasted carrot and onion soup, 76
Roasted red pepper
   bisque with garlic boats, 75
   soup with red curry and coconut milk, 71
   and zucchini soup, 74
Roasted sweet potato soup with orange crème fraîche, 134
Roasted tomato bisque, 138
Romano beans
   chili and corn soup, 122
   and pasta soup, 54
   Tex-Mex soup, 173
Romano cheese curls, 72
Rouille, hot pepper, 39
Rye croutons, 30

S

Sahara snacks, 36
Salmon steak, and smoked salmon chowder, 98
Salsa topping, 33
Salt lover's crunchy wedges, 32
Sausage. *See also* Italian sausage
   lamb, barley chowder, 88
   savoy soup, 81
Scallops
   chowder with smoked bacon, 90
   seafood chowder, 102
   watercress soup with, 129
Scotch broth, 60
Seafood chowder, 102
Seeds, toasted, 111
Seeing-double soup, 132
Sherry, mushroom chowder with Swiss cheese, 93
Shortbreads, Parmesan, 42
Shrimp
   bisque, 56
   bouillabaisse, 58
   chowder, 100, 102
   gazpacho, 51
   New Orleans gumbo, 178
   pumpkin soup with, 112

seafood chowder, 102
Thai-style chowder, 100
Smoked salmon, and salmon steak chowder, 98
Snacks, Sahara, 36
Snow peas, chicken soup with, 128
Sole velouté with diced vegetables, 142
Spicy lime butter coins, 41
Spicy roasted red pepper bisque, 75
Spicy Thai chowder with shrimp and coconut milk, 100
Spinach
   and beans in broth, 82
   chicken soup with, 128
   and chickpea soup, 80
   soup with nutmeg and yogurt, 79
   and tortellini soup, 165
   watercress and scallop soup, 129
Split peas, green
   and prosciutto soup, 125
Split peas, yellow
   French Canadian pea soup, 61
   Scotch broth, 60
Squash
   and cider soup, 110
   and Granny Smith apple soup, 171
   seeing double soup, 132
   soup with shrimp, 112
Stock, 16–27. *See also* Court bouillon
   beef, 22
   chicken, 16
   chicken-bone, 20
   cooked poultry, 18
   fish, 25
   ham bone, 21
   to clarify, 23
   veal, 22
   vegetable, 26, 27
Sweet onions. *See also* Onions
   French onion soup, 50
   and tomato soup with basil crème, 83
Sweet potatoes, roasted, soup with crème fraîche, 134

Swiss chard, chicken soup with, 128
Swiss cheese, and mushroom chowder, 93

T

Tex-Mex chili soup, 173
Thyme, and parsley pick-ups, 38
Tomato(es)
   and basil soup with olive oil, 149
   Cajun soup, 172
   with cayenne mayonnaise soup, 65
   clam chowder, 97
   lentil soup, 108
   and mussel soup, 174
   salsa, 33
   sweet onion soup with basil crème, 83
   with tortellini soup, 164
Tortellini
   and spinach soup, 165
   tomato soup with, 164
Tubettini, and bean soup, 54
Turkey, cooked, stock, 18

V

Veal, stock, 22
Vegetable(s)
   barley chowder with lamb sausage, 88
   and clam soup, 136
   cream soup, 169
   dark stock, 27
   Finnish soup, 66
   light stock, 26
   minestrone, 52
   oven-roasted, soup, 70
   sausage savoy soup, 81
   sole velouté with, 142
   stock, 26, 27
   summer soup with Romano curls, 72
Vichyssoise
   Dijon, 46
   parsnip, 47
Vietnamese pho soup, 176

W

Watercress
  with cucumber raita soup,
    150
  with scallops soup, 129
White bean soup with barley,
  123
Whole wheat croutons, 30
Wieners, and corn chowder,
  92
Wild mushroom, and wild rice
  chowder, 94

Wild rice
  cooking technique, 95
  and wild mushroom
    chowder, 94
Winter barley chowder with
  lamb sausage, 88
Winter squash, with toasted
  seeds soup, 111

Y

Yeast, about, 43
Yeast breads, focaccia, 43

Yellow bell peppers, with fresh
  tomato salsa, 152
Yogurt
  avocado soup, 154
  cucumber soup, 182
  spinach soup with, 79

Z

Zippy crunchy wedges,
  32
Zucchini, and roasted red
  pepper soup, 74

More Great Books
from Robert Rose

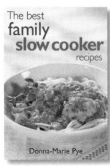

Appliance Cooking

- 125 Best Microwave Oven Recipes
  by Johanna Burkhard
- The Blender Bible
  by Andrew Chase and Nicole Young
- The Mixer Bible
  by Meredith Deeds and Carla Snyder
- The 150 Best Slow Cooker Recipes
  by Judith Finlayson
- Delicious & Dependable Slow Cooker Recipes
  by Judith Finlayson
- 125 Best Vegetarian Slow Cooker Recipes
  by Judith Finlayson
- 125 Best Rotisserie Oven Recipes
  by Judith Finlayson
- 125 Best Food Processor Recipes
  by George Geary
- The Best Family Slow Cooker Recipes
  by Donna-Marie Pye
- The Best Convection Oven Cookbook
  by Linda Stephen
- 125 Best Toaster Oven Recipes
  by Linda Stephen
- 250 Best American Bread Machine Baking Recipes
  by Donna Washburn and Heather Butt
- 250 Best Canadian Bread Machine Baking Recipes
  by Donna Washburn and Heather Butt

Baking

- 250 Best Cakes & Pies
  by Esther Brody
- 500 Best Cookies, Bars & Squares
  by Esther Brody
- 500 Best Muffin Recipes
  by Esther Brody
- 125 Best Cheesecake Recipes
  by George Geary
- 125 Best Chocolate Recipes
  by Julie Hasson
- 125 Best Chocolate Chip Recipes
  by Julie Hasson
- 125 Best Cupcake Recipes
  by Julie Hasson
- Complete Cake Mix Magic
  by Jill Snider

Healthy Cooking

- 125 Best Vegetarian Recipes
  by Byron Ayanoglu with contributions from Algis Kemezys
- America's Best Cookbook for Kids with Diabetes
  by Colleen Bartley
- Canada's Best Cookbook for Kids with Diabetes
  by Colleen Bartley
- The Juicing Bible
  by Pat Crocker and Susan Eagles
- The Smoothies Bible
  by Pat Crocker

- 125 Best Vegan Recipes
  by Maxine Effenson Chuck and Beth Gurney
- 500 Best Healthy Recipes
  Edited by Lynn Roblin, RD
- 125 Best Gluten-Free Recipes
  by Donna Washburn and Heather Butt
- The Best Gluten-Free Family Cookbook
  by Donna Washburn and Heather Butt
- America's Everyday Diabetes Cookbook
  Edited by Katherine E. Younker, MBA, RD
- Canada's Everyday Diabetes Choice Recipes
  Edited by Katherine E. Younker, MBA, RD
- Canada's Complete Diabetes Cookbook
  Edited by Katherine E. Younker, MBA, RD
- The Best Diabetes Cookbook (U.S.)
  Edited by Katherine E. Younker, MBA, RD
- The Best Low-Carb Cookbook
  from Robert Rose

Recent Bestsellers

- 125 Best Soup Recipes
  by Marylin Crowley and Joan Mackie
- The Convenience Cook
  by Judith Finlayson
- 125 Best Ice Cream Recipes
  by Marilyn Linton and Tanya Linton

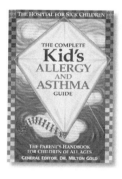

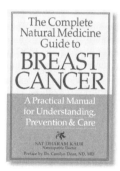

- Easy Indian Cooking
  by Suneeta Vaswani
- Simply Thai Cooking
  by Wandee Young and Byron Ayanoglu

Health

- The Complete Natural Medicine Guide to the 50 Most Common Medicinal Herbs
  by Dr. Heather Boon, B.Sc.Phm., Ph.D., and Michael Smith, B.Pharm, M.R.Pharm.S., ND
- The Complete Kid's Allergy and Asthma Guide
  Edited by Dr. Milton Gold
- The Complete Natural Medicine Guide to Breast Cancer
  by Sat Dharam Kaur, ND
- The Complete Doctor's Stress Solution
  by Penny Kendall-Reed, MSc, ND, and Dr. Stephen Reed, MD, FRCSC
- The Complete Doctor's Healthy Back Bible
  by Dr. Stephen Reed, MD, and Penny Kendall-Reed, MSc, ND, with Dr. Michael Ford, MD, FRCSC, and Dr. Charles Gregory, MD, ChB, FRCP(C)
- Everyday Risks in Pregnancy & Breastfeeding
  by Dr. Gideon Koren, MD, FRCP(C), ND
- Help for Eating Disorders
  by Dr. Debra Katzman, MD, FRCP(C), and Dr. Leora Pinhas, MD